POCKET
ATLAS

POCKET

ATLAS

PHILIP STEELE

p

Editor: Sean Connolly
Design: Geoff Sida
Cover Design: David West • Children's Books
Cartographic Editor: Keith Lye
Project Manager: Kate Miles
Production Assistant: Ian Paulyn
Editorial Assistant: Lynne French

This is a Parragon Book
This edition published in 2000

Parragon
Queen Street House
4 Queen Street
Bath BA1 1HE, UK

Produced by Miles Kelly Publishing Ltd
Bardfield Centre, Great Bardfield, Essex CM7 4SL

British Library Cataloguing-in-Publication Data

A catalogue record for this book is
available from the British Library.

ISBN 0-75253-150-6

Printed in Italy

CONTENTS

HOW TO USE THIS ATLAS

Welcome to the planet Earth! The maps in this atlas show the world we live in. Maps are plans which show the surface of the world as if it were flat, instead of round.

Maps often show the lie of the land and may include mountains, rivers and seas. Maps which only show these kind of details are called 'physical'. Maps which only show the borders of countries, states, counties or provinces are

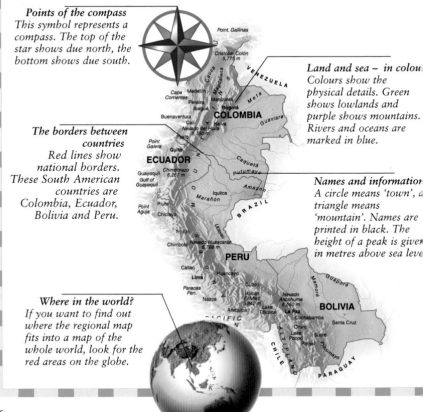

Points of the compass
This symbol represents a compass. The top of the star shows due north, the bottom shows due south.

Land and sea – in colou
Colours show the physical details. Green shows lowlands and purple shows mountains. Rivers and oceans are marked in blue.

The borders between countries
Red lines show national borders. These South American countries are Colombia, Ecuador, Bolivia and Peru.

Names and informatio
A circle means 'town', a triangle means 'mountain'. Names are printed in black. The height of a peak is give in metres above sea leve

Where in the world?
If you want to find out where the regional map fits into a map of the whole world, look for the red areas on the globe.

6

called 'political'. The maps in this book show the physical details of the land, but they show national borders and major cities as well.

How do you find the place you are looking for? First of all look up the name you want in the index on p.123. When you have found the right page, look for the name on the map of the region. The little round maps help you to see at a glance which part of the world is being shown. The words will tell you about the countries, the climate of the region and the plants that grow there, the peoples and how they live.

MAKING MAPS

The world is three-dimensional, which means that it can only be shown accurately on a globe. Map-makers have had to work out clever ways of representing the Earth's curves on flat surfaces such as sheets of paper or computer screens. Some of these methods, called projections, are shown here.

◄ *This projection shows the world in segments as though the map has been peeled off the globe. The shapes always get a bit stretched and distorted when the round world is projected onto a flat surface.*

▲ *Gerardus Mercator in 1538 was the first to depict the world on a flat surface.*

▲ *Peters' projection tries to show the sizes of different countries in proportion to each other.*

WORLD FACTS

The Earth is a huge ball of rock and metal, spinning around in space. A line drawn around the middle, or Equator, would measure 40,008 kilometres. The planet's surface covers an area of about 510,000,000 square kilometres, of which 71 per cent is covered by sea.

Earth Extremes

The lowest exposed part of Earth's surface is in southwest Asia, beside the Dead Sea, at 400 metres below sea level.

The world's deepest lake is Baikal, in the Russian Federation. It plunges to 1,637 metres.

About 565 kilometres of caves and underground passages have been explored in the Mammoth National Park, Kentucky, USA – the world's biggest system.

At 446 kilometres, the Grand Canyon is the world's longest gorge. It was carved out by the Colorado River in the southwestern United States.

The Ring of Fire is the name given to the borders of the Pacific Ocean, because so many dangerous volcanoes are sited there.

Highest Mountains

Everest or Qomolongma, is a spectacular peak in Tibet, on the border between China and Nepal. At 8,840 metres it is higher above sea level than any other mountain.

Mauna Kea, on the Pacific island of Hawaii, measures 10,205 metres from the ocean floor to its peak, which rise to 4,205 metres above sea level.

The highest active volcano in the world rises on the border between Argentina and Chile. It is Ojos del Salado, 6,887 metres high.

The highest range of mountains on any continent is the Himalaya-Karakoram, which includes Everest and 13 other peaks over 8,000 metres.

AND FIGURES

Longest Rivers

The River Nile flows from Central Africa to the Mediterranean Sea, through the deserts of Egypt. Its natural course is 6,670 kilometres long.

The River Amazon could be longer than the Nile – it all depends just where you start and finish measuring, for the river has several mouths. It is normally reckoned to be 6,448 kilometres long. It drains the world's largest surviving area of rainforest.

There is no doubt about which river is in third place. The Chang Jiang (or Yangtze) flows 6,300 kilometres across central China.

A delta is an area where a river splits into separate waterways before flowing into the ocean. The Ganges-Brahmaputra delta, on the Bay of Bengal, covers about 75,000 square kilometres.

Oceans

The biggest ocean in the world is the Pacific, with a surface area of 166,241,700 square kilometres. It is bordered by Asia and Australia to the west and the Americas to the east.

The deepest sea is in the Pacific Ocean. The Marianas Trench, a deep crack in the ocean floor, plunges to a depth of 10,911 metres.

Deserts

The Sahara is the world's biggest desert, covering about 7,700,000 square kilometres. It stretches right across North Africa and takes in burning hot sand dunes, beds of gravel and rocks.

The driest place on Earth is probably Chile's Atacama desert, which has almost no rain at any time.

Major Waterfalls

The Angel Falls, or Churun-Meru, have the biggest drop in the world, totalling 979 metres. They are in Venezuela, in South America.

The Boyoma Falls, in the Democratic Republic of the Congo, Africa, are the most powerful in the world. They average 17,000 cubic metres of water per second.

Chukchi
Sea

Beaufort
Sea

Bering Strait

GREENLAND

Baffin Bay

Arctic Circle

Davis Strait

Denmark Strait

ICELAND

Hudson Bay

CANADA

IRELAND

Gulf of
Alaska

Newfoundland

ALEUTIAN ISLANDS

UNITED STATES OF AMERICA

NORTH

ATLANTIC

OCEAN

PORTUGAL

MOROCCO

CANARY
ISLANDS

Gulf of Mexico

Tropic of Cancer

WESTERN
SAHARA

HAWAIIAN ISLANDS

MEXICO

BAHAMAS

CUBA

DOMINICAN
REPUBLIC

W
E
S
T

I
N
D
I
E
S

JAMAICA HAITI

PUERTO RICO

MAURITANIA

BELIZE

Caribbean Sea

SENEGAL

GUATEMALA HONDURAS

GAMBIA
GUINEA-BISSAU

GUINEA

EL SALVADOR NICARAGUA

COSTA RICA

TRINIDAD &
TOBAGO

SIERRA LEONE

IV
CO

LIBERIA

PANAMA

VENEZUELA

GUYANA

SURINAM

FRENCH GUIANA

COLOMBIA

Equator

GALAPAGOS
ISLANDS

ECUADOR

SOUTH

PERU

BRAZIL

ATLANTIC

OCEAN

BOLIVIA

PARAGUAY

Tropic of Capricorn

CHILE

URUGUAY

ARGENTINA

FALKLAND/MALVINAS
ISLANDS

South Georgia

Antarctic Circle

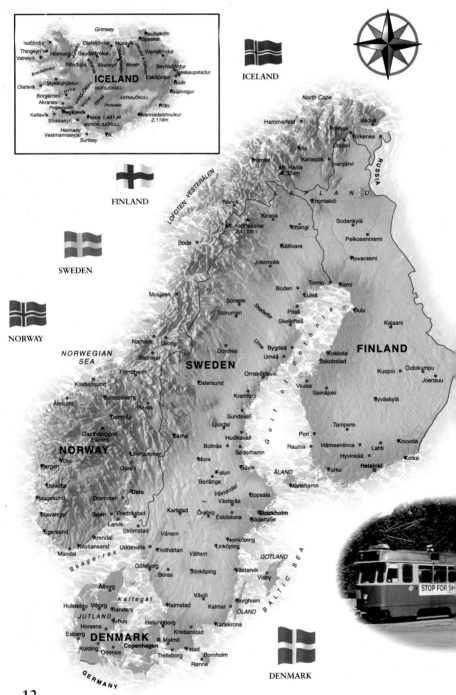

ICELAND

ICELAND

Grimsey
Raufarhöfn
Ísafjördur · Olafsfjördur · Húsavík · Kopasker
Thingeyri · Hólmavík · Saudárkrókur · Vopnafjördur
Vatneyri · Blönduós · Akureyri · Mývatn · Seyhisfjördur
Breidafjördur · Stykkishólmur · Eskifjördur · Neskaupstadur
Olafsvik · Hvítá · HOFSJÖKULL · Búdir
Borgarnes · Hríta · Pjörsá · VATNAJÖKULL · Djúpivogur
Akranes · Pingvallavatn · Porisvatn · Höfn
Keflavík · **Reykjavík** · Hekla 1,491 m · Hvannadalshnúkur
Stokkseyri · MYRDALSJÖKULL · 2,119m
Heimaey · Vík
Vestmannaeyjar · Surtsey

FINLAND

SWEDEN

NORWAY

North Cape
Hammerfest · Porsak · Vadso
Kirkenes
Alta · Utsjoki
Tromso · Karasjok · Inarijärvi
Mt. Haltia · 1,324m · RUSSIA
Narvik · LAPLAND · Enontekiö
Kiruna
Mt. Kebnekaise · Vittangi · Sodankylä
2,111m
Bodø · Gällivare · Pelkosenniemi
Jokkmokk · Rovaniemi

NORWEGIAN
SEA
Mosjøen · Sorsele · Boden · Tornio · Kemi
Storuman · Skellefte · Piteå · Oulu
Skellefteå
Kajaani
Namsos · Grong · Bygdeå · Kokkola
Steinkjer · Dorotea · Umeå · Jakobstad · FINLAND
Trondheim · **SWEDEN** · Ornsköldsvik · Kuopio · Outokumpu
Kristiansund · Östersund · Vaasa · Joensuu
Sunndalsøra · Kramfors · Seinäjoki · Jyväskylä
Ålesund · Røros
Dombås · Sundsvall · Tampere
Galdhøpiggen · Ljusdal · Pori · Hämeenlinna · Kouvola
2,469m · Särna · Hudiksvall · Rauma · Lahti · Kotka
NORWAY · Bollnäs · Söderhamn · Hyvinkää
Voss · Lillehammer · Mora · Helsinki
Bergen · Gjøvik · Falun · Gävle · ÅLAND · Turku
Uskedal · Borlänge · Mariehamn
Haugesund · Drammen · Västerdal · Uppsala
Stavanger · Skien · Fredrikstad · Karlstad · Örebro · Västerås · **Stockholm**
Egersund · Larvik · Strömstad · Eskilstuna · Södertälje
Arendal · Vänern · Norrköping
Mandal · Kristiansand · Uddevalla · Trollhättan · Linköping
Skagerrak · Vättern · GOTLAND
Göteborg · Jönköping · Västervik
Boras · Visby
Ålborg · Kattegat · Växjö · Borgholm
Holstebro · Viborg · Randers · Halmstad · Kalmar · ÖLAND
JUTLAND · Horsens · Århus · Helsingborg · Karlskrona
Esbjerg · **DENMARK** · Kristianstad
Kolding · Malmö
Odense · **Copenhagen** · Ystad
Trelleborg · Bornholm
GERMANY · Rønne

BALTIC SEA

Gulf of Bothnia

DENMARK

STOP FOR S

THE FAR NORTH

The lands of Europe's far north include the Scandinavian countries of Denmark, Sweden and Norway. Finland lies to the east and Iceland far to the west, in the North Atlantic Ocean. All these countries except Denmark border the Arctic Circle, but their waters are warmed by ocean currents.

Two large peninsulas stick out from the mainland of northwestern Europe, like the pincers of a giant crab. They divide the North Sea from the Baltic. The southern peninsula is the smaller one, which extends northwards from Germany. It is called Jutland. Together with the nearby islands of Fyn, Lolland, Falster and Sjælland it makes up the kingdom of Denmark. Most of Denmark is flat and low-lying, a country of green farmland. The Danish capital, Copenhagen, is on Sjælland and is home to over 1.3 million people. A further 4 million Danes live in the rest of this small country. Denmark exports bacon and dairy products. This is the most southerly Scandinavian country, with the mildest climate. Denmark also rules the Faeroe Islands and distant Greenland, although these territories now have their own parliaments

◀ *Taking a tram ride*
A tram squeals through the streets of Helsinki, the Finnish capital. Trams are still a popular means of transport in many northern European cities.

and make their own laws.

Across the windy channels of Skagerrak and Kattegat, between the North Sea and the Baltic, is the long Scandinavian peninsula, which stretches northwards beyond the Arctic Circle. The landscape of this part of Europe was shaped by movements of ice in prehistoric times. Glaciers carved out the deep sea inlets called fiords along the ragged western coast. Ranges of mountains run down the Scandinavian peninsula like a backbone. They descend to a land of spruce and birch forests, bogs and thousands of sparkling lakes. Scandinavia is the home of reindeer, elk, brown bear and salmon.

Summers can be warm, but winters are bitterly cold, with heavy snow. Cross-country skiing and other winter sports are popular. In Arctic regions the midsummer sun shines through much of the night, while the days of midwinter are dark, lit up only by the eerie flickering of the northern lights, known as aurora borealis, in the sky.

Norway occupies the western half of the Scandinavian peninsula. This is a harsh landscape with few resources apart from timber and water, so the Norwegians have always had to turn seawards to survive. They live by fishing, and North Sea production platforms also make Norway the largest producer of oil and natural gas in western Europe. The Norwegian capital, Oslo, lies in the south of the country. The population of the country as a whole is 4.4 million. Norway's North Cape, or Nordkapp, is the northernmost point in the whole of Europe. Norway also rules two Arctic territories – Jan Mayen island and the Svalbard archipelago.

Sweden occupies the eastern and southern part of the Scandinavian peninsula, with its capital at Stockholm. This city is an old trading port built over islands linked by bridges. Sweden has the highest population of these northern lands, at 8.9 million. It is a major exporter of timber, paper, wooden furniture and motor vehicles. It uses its rivers to power hydroelectric schemes and has reserves of iron ore, copper, silver and uranium. The southern part of the country has fertile farmland which produces grain and root crops.

Iceland is an independent country with strong

◄ Copenhagen's Little Mermaid
This statue at the water's edge shows a character made famous over a hundred years ago by Danish fairy tale writer Hans Christian Andersen.

historical links to mainland Scandinavia. It is a sparsely populated island of bleak moors, mountains, glaciers and snow fields, volcanoes, warm springs and geysers – spouts of water which gush up from underground. Many Icelanders live by fishing and by farming. The same energy which heats the island's hot springs provides power to heat homes and greenhouses, where vegetables and flowers can be grown.

Today's Danes, Swedes, Norwegians and Icelanders are all closely related, and so are the

◄ Fiords of the Vikings
Snow-capped mountains and sheer rocks plunge into the still, deep waters of Nordfiord, near the Norwegian village of Hopland.

▲ *Hand weaving in Småland*
A weaver works at her loom in the Småland region of southern Sweden. All the Scandinavian countries have a long tradition of arts and crafts.

various Germanic languages that they speak. It was from Scandinavia that the seafarers known as Vikings set out about 1,200 years ago. The Vikings raided and settled the coasts of Western Europe, traded in Russia and the Middle East, settled Iceland and Greenland and even reached North America.

Not all northern Europeans are descended from the Vikings. The Arctic lands of northern Scandinavia are known as Lapland and are home to the Saami, a people who traditionally led nomadic lives, following their herds of reindeer to their pastures. Some are still herders, while others have found more settled work.

The 5 million Finns are not

related to any of the other peoples in the region. Finland borders the Russian Federation and has coasts on the Gulf of Bothnia and the Gulf of Finland, which are long arms of the Baltic Sea. It has thousands of lakes and its evergreen forests make it a leading producer of wood pulp and paper. Helsinki is the northernmost capital on the European mainland. Finland was ruled by Sweden in the Middle

▲ *Marching through Copenhagen*
Young members of the Tivoli Guard Marching Band parade through the Tivoli Gardens. They wear red and white, the Danish national colours.

Ages, and by Russia from 1809 until 1917.

Most of the peoples of Europe's far north are Lutheran Christians. Denmark, Norway and Sweden are all monarchies, ruled by kings or queens. Finland and Iceland are both republics. Denmark, Sweden and Finland are trading partners within the European Union (EU), but Norway voted against joining this economic and political alliance in 1994.

ST LUCIA'S DAY
In the dark days of the Scandinavian winter, many festivals are held which celebrate light and warmth. St Lucia, or Lucy, is the Christian saint of light. Her feast day is 13 December and it is celebrated in Sweden by girls wearing candles and wreathes of green leaves on their heads.

West Frisian Islands
Ameland
Terschelling
Vlieland
Leeuwarden
Groningen
Texel
Waddenzee
Sneek
Assen
Barrier Dam
Emmer
IJsselmeer
North-East
Polder
Meppel
Alkmaar
Markerwaard
Polder
(planned)
Flevoland
Polder
Zwolle
Zaanstad
NETHERLANDS
Almelo
Haarlem
Amsterdam
Ensch
Hilversum
IJssel
Leiden
Amersfoort
Apeldoorn
Gouda
Utrecht
The Hague
Lek
Delft
Arnhem
Rotterdam
Nijmegen
GERMANY
Dordrecht
Waal
Maas
's-Hertogenbosch
Oosterschelde
Breda
Tilburg
Vlissingen
Eindhoven
Westerschelde
Venlo
Zeebrugge
Ostend
Bruges
Antwerp
St. Niklaas
Ghent
Genk
Roeslare
Mechelen
Hasselt
Heerlen
Kortijk
Aalst
Brussels
Leuven
(Louvain)
Maastricht
Waterloo
Liège
Vaalserberg
321m
BELGIUM
Huy
Meuse
Verviers
Tournai
La Louvière
Sambre
Namur
Spa
Botrange
694m
Mons
Charleroi
FRANCE
Dinant
ARDENNES
MOUNTAINS
Buurgplatz
559m
Bastogne
GERMANY
Libramont
LUXEMBOURG
Luxembourg
Esch-sur-Alzette

NETHERLANDS

BELGIUM

LOW COUNTRIES

B etween Germany and France, the North Sea coast is made up of sand dunes, islands and estuaries. The land is very low and at the mercy of storms and severe flooding. The flat fields of the Netherlands and Belgium rise in the south to the Ardennes hills and the little country of Luxembourg.

The country of the Netherlands is sometimes called Holland, but that is really the name of just two of its provinces, North and South Holland. 'Nether' means 'low' and this is the lowest, flattest part of northern Europe. Long barriers and sea defences have been built to protect the countryside from North Sea floods. Large areas of land called polders have been reclaimed from the sea over the ages. The Dutch landscape is

green, criss-crossed by canals and dykes, tree-lined roads and bridges and modern motorways. Many old windmills, which were built to pump the polders dry, may still be seen.

After a period under Spanish rule, the Netherlands became wealthy in the 1600s by trading with Southeast Asia. Its capital city, Amsterdam, still has many beautiful old houses and canals dating back to this golden age. Amsterdam is a lively city which attracts young people from all over Europe. It is ringed by modern suburbs. There are many other fine old towns and cities. The Dutch have a long tradition of art and design. The work of painters such as Rembrandt van Rijn (1606-69) and

◄ Beside the North Sea
The seafaring tradition of the Netherlands dates back to the 1600s. This is the old harbour at Hoorn in North Holland.

Vincent van Gogh (1853-90) may be seen in museums and galleries.

The Netherlands today remain a centre of commerce, exporting beers, tulips and other bulbs, cut flowers, tomatoes and vegetables as well

▲ *Old times remembered*
Traditional costume may still be seen at festivals in some coastal regions and islands of the Netherlands.

as dairy products, especially cheese. Industry is concentrated in the south, producing electrical and household goods. The city of Rotterdam is the world's busiest seaport.

Dutch people make up the biggest part of the population, which numbers about 15.6 million. In the far north and on offshore islands are the closely related Frisian people, who have their own language. The country is also home to many people whose families came from former Dutch colonies in Indonesia and Surinam, as well as immigrants from Turkey and southern Europe. The majority of people are Christians, belonging to both the Roman Catholic and Protestant traditions.

The Flemish people of Belgium are closely related to the Dutch and their two languages are very similar. Belgium is also home to a French-speaking people, the Walloons, who mostly live in the south of the country. Language and cultural differences have given rise to conflict between the two communities over the years. Both Flemish and French are official languages. The total population of Belgium is about 10.2 million. Most Belgians are Roman Catholics.

The north of the country is densely populated, with the capital centrally located at Brussels. Much of the Belgian countryside is also very low and flat, with large areas of polder. It is crossed by the rivers Schelde (also known as Escaut or Scheldt), Meuse (or Maas) and Sambre. The land rises to the south, where the wooded hills of the Ardennes rise above old stone-built towns and villages.

Belgium is heavily industrialized, producing steel, chemicals, plastics, paints and fertilizers. It was formerly an important coal-mining region. The country is also known for its fine foods. Chocolates, pâtés, spicy sausages, hams and

traditional strong beers are all exported. Ghent and Bruges have produced textiles since the Middle Ages.

Luxembourg is a tiny country, a survivor of the age when most of Europe was divided into little states, principalities and duchies. However, modern industry and banking have made Luxembourg the wealthiest country in Europe. The Ardennes cross its northern region, while the south is rich farmland. In the east, on the German border, are the steeply banked vineyards of the Moselle valley. The people of Luxembourg speak French, German and a local language called Letzebuergesch.

Belgium and the Netherlands are both monarchies and Luxembourg is ruled by a Grand Duke. The three countries have close ties. In 1948, after the terrible years of the Second World War (1939-45), Belgium, the Netherlands and Luxembourg set up an economic union called 'Benelux'. It prospered and in 1957 they went on to become

▼ Theme park
Hurtling through the water, these children enjoy getting soaked on the Rada river at Alibi fun park, Belgium.

three of the six countries which founded what is now the European Union (EU). Many EU organizations are now based in the region. Brussels, the Belgian capital, is headquarters of the EU Council and Commission, and Luxembourg City is the home of the European Court of Justice and the secretariat of the European Parliament.

▼ Sails in the wind
The sails of windmills rise from the flat, green farmland of South Holland, at Stompwijk near Gouda.

THE FEAR OF FLOODS
Nearly 2,000 people died along the coast of the Netherlands in 1953, when the North Sea storms caused dreadful flooding. The engineers' answer to tragedies such as this was the Delta Project, which was completed in 1986. It was decided to dam three river mouths and to build a huge barrier, 9 kilometres in length, across the East Scheldt river. Today, whenever the sea levels rise, 62 steel gates are raised against the floods.

▶ **Wren**
This tiny bird, with its distinctive cocked tail, can be seen all over Great Britain.

SHETLAND ISLANDS
Yell   Unst
Foula   Lerwick
Sumburgh Head
Fair Isle

NORTH SEA

SCOTLAND

Westray
ORKNEY ISLANDS
Kirkwall
Cape Wrath   Hoy   South Ronaldsay
Butt of Lewis   John o'Groats
Thurso
Stornoway
Lewis   North Minch
OUTER HEBRIDES
North Uist   NORTH WEST HIGHLANDS
Fraserburgh
Moray Firth   Peterhead
Skye   Inverness
South Uist   Loch Ness   Spey   Don
INNER HEBRIDES   Dee   Aberdeen
Barra   Rhum   Mallaig
Ben Nevis ▲   GRAMPIAN MTS.
Coll   1,343 m
Tiree   Mull   Oban   SIDLAW HILLS   Montrose
Jura   Loch   Perth   Tay   Dundee
Lomond   OCHIL HILLS
Greenock   Forth   Firth of Forth
Islay   Glasgow   Edinburgh   St Abbs Head
SCOTLAND   Berwick-upon-Tweed
Kilmarnock   Clyde   Holy I.
Arran   Ayr   Jedburgh   Tweed
Kintyre Pen.   SOUTHERN UPLANDS
CHEVIOT HILLS

NORTHERN IRELAND

Malin Head   NORTH
Tory I.   Rathlin I.   Giants   Newcastle upon Tyne
Aran I.   Londonderry   Causeway   ANTRIM   Dumfries   Tyne   Sunderland
DONEGAL   SPERRIN   MTS.   Stranraer   Carlisle   Durham
MTS.   MTS.   Lough   Solway   PENNINES   Middlesbrough
Erris Head   Donegal Bay   Donegal   Neagh   Firth   Lake   NORTH YORK   Scarborough
Achill Head   Lower Lough   Belfast   District   MOORS
Lough   Erne   Scafell Pike   Flamborough Head
Conn   Sligo   Upper Lough   Armagh   Isle of Man   978 m   Swale
Clew   Lough   Erne   Slieve Donard   Douglas   Walney I.   Leeds   York
Bay   Allen   852 m   Morecambe Bay   Kingston upon Hull
Lough   Dundalk   Blackpool   Bradford   Spurn Head
Mask   Lough Ree   Boyne   IRISH   Preston   Oldham
Lough   SEA   Wigan   Manchester   LINCOLN
Corrib   Athlone   Liffey   Dublin   Anglesey   Liverpool   Sheffield   WOLDS
Galway   IRELAND   BOG OF   Holyhead   Rotherham
Galway Bay   Lough Derg   ALLEN   Dun Laoghaire   Llandudno   Wrexham   Derby   Nottingham   The
ARAN ISLANDS   Carlow   WICKLOW   Caernarfon   Snowdon   ENGLAND   Wash
Loop Head   Shannon   Nore   MTS.   Wicklow   Bay   1,085 m   Stoke on Trent   Leicester   THE FENS   Norwich
Limerick   Barrow   Head   Bardsey I.   CAMBRIAN MTS.   Wolverhampton   Welland   Peterborough   EAST
Tipperary   Cardigan   Walsall   ANGLIA
GALTY MTS.   Waterford   Bay   Birmingham   Coventry   Northampton   Cambridge
Gt. Blasket I.   Killarney   Blackwater   Wexford   Aberystwyth   WALES   Wye   Milton Keynes   Ipsw
Dingle Bay   Carrauntoohil   Hook   Cardigan   Cheltenham   Oxford   Luton   Colche
1,041 m   Cork   Head   Carmarthen   COTSWOLD HILLS   CHILTERNS
Kenmare River   Bantry   St. Brides   Gloucester   Swindon   London   Chelmsford
Bantry Bay   Old Head of Kinsale   Bay   Swansea   Newport   Severn   Reading   Thames   Southend-on-
Mizen   Milford Haven   Gower   Cardiff   Bristol   Basingstoke   NORTH DOWNS   Canterbu
Head   Peninsula   Bristol Channel   MENDIP   HAMPSHIRE   THE WEALD   Folkest
WALES   Lundy   HILLS   Salisbury   DOWNS   SOUTH DOWNS
Ilfracombe   Bridgwater   Winchester   Hastings
EXMOOR   Southampton   Portsmouth   Brighton
REPUBLIC OF   Bude   Bournemouth   Isle of Wight   ENGLISH CHANNEL
IRELAND   DARTMOOR   Exeter   Portland Bill
St. Ives   Torbay   Lyme Bay
ISLES OF   Penzance   Plymouth
SCILLY   Lands   Lizard Point
End

ATLANTIC OCEAN

NORTH CHANNEL

ENGLAND

Alderney
CHANNEL ISLANDS
Guernsey
Jersey

BRITISH ISLES

The British Isles lie off the northwestern coast of Europe, between the shallow waters of the North Sea and the stormy Atlantic Ocean. Their western shores are warmed by an ocean current called the North Atlantic Drift. The climate is mild, with a high rainfall in the west.

The largest of the British Isles is called Great Britain, and its three countries (England, Scotland and Wales) are joined within the United Kingdom (UK). The second largest of the British Isles is Ireland. Most of Ireland is an independent republic, but part of the north is governed as a province of the United Kingdom.

Several islands off the shore of Great Britain are self-governing, but have the British monarch as head of state and close political links with the UK. These include the Channel Islands, off the coast of France, and the Isle of Man in the Irish Sea.

About 80 per cent of the UK population lives in England, the largest of the three countries within the United Kingdom. It takes up the southern part of

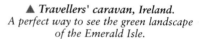
▲ *Travellers' caravan, Ireland.*
A perfect way to see the green landscape of the Emerald Isle.

Great Britain. The southeast is densely populated and includes the city of London, on the River Thames. London is the capital and has a population of over 8 million. The chief shopping districts and the Houses of Parliament lie in the west, while the City district to the east is a centre of business and finance.

England's south coast takes in the grasslands of the Salisbury Plains and the major ports of Southampton, Portsmouth and Plymouth. In the southwest, the long rocky peninsula of Cornwall extends towards

▼ *Historical towns and villages*
Half-timbered houses may still be seen at Stratford-upon-Avon, the home town of the great English playwright William Shakespeare (1564-1616).

the Scilly Islands in the Atlantic Ocean. The flat lowlands of East Anglia produce wheat and vegetables, while the Midlands are mostly industrial. Birmingham is the second largest city in the UK. Northern England is dominated by the hill country of the Pennines and the Yorkshire moors and by the lakes of Cumbria. Major northern ports include Liverpool in the west and Newcastle upon Tyne in the east.

Wales is a land of mountains and uplands, which descend through green valleys to coastal lowlands. It raises sheep and cattle. The large Welsh coal mining and slate quarrying industries have declined, but have been replaced to some extent by factories producing electronics and consumer goods. The capital is Cardiff, in the industrial southeast.

Scotland has the highest mountain ranges of the British Isles, fertile lowlands and long lakes, or lochs. Offshore are many island chains, including the Hebrides and the Orkneys. The capital is Edinburgh, in the east. It is dominated by a high castle, and is famous for its international arts festival. Glasgow is Scotland's largest city, an industrial centre on the River Clyde.

Ireland is a less crowded island than Great Britain. It has rolling green fields, expanses of peat bog, misty hills, lakes and rivers. In the west, steep cliffs are pounded by Atlantic breakers. The capital of the Irish Republic, Dublin, lies in the east of the country, on the River Liffey. It is an attractive city with many fine houses from the 1700s and 1800s. The Northern Irish capital is the industrial city of Belfast.

▲ *Harvest time in the wheat fields*
The landscapes of the British Isles have been shaped by thousands of years of farming. Food products are major exports from both Great Britain and Ireland.

▶ *Conwy castle, North Wales*
The Welsh fought against English and Norman invaders for over 800 years. This massive castle was built by their fiercest enemy, the English King Edward I, in the 1280s.

◀ **Loch Awe, in western Scotland**
This is the longest freshwater loch in Scotland, lying beneath the mountain of Ben Cruachan and the ruins of Kilchurn Castle.

▼ **The heart of London**
Piccadilly Circus lies at the heart of London's West End. Its famous statue is meant to be an angel, but is better known as Eros (the Greek god of love).

It was in the British Isles that the Industrial Revolution – the age of factories and machines – first started in the 1700s and 1800s. Today both the United Kingdom and Ireland are members of the European Union (EU). Farming is important throughout the British Isles, but service industries such as banking, insurance and tourism have largely overtaken manufacturing. Resources include rich oilfields in the North Sea.

English is spoken throughout the British Isles, but other languages may be heard too – Welsh, Irish and Scots Gaelic, and the various languages spoken by British people of Asian and African descent. The Welsh, Cornish, Scots and Irish are mostly of Celtic descent, while many of the English are descended from Anglo-Saxons, a Germanic people who invaded England about 1,500 years ago.

In the Middle Ages, England came to dominate its neighbours in the British Isles. Together they went on to rule the largest overseas empire the world has ever seen. In the 1900s the British Empire rapidly declined. Nearer to home, Ireland started on the road to independence in 1921, although continuing British rule in the north caused a violent conflict which survives today. Both Scotland and Wales voted in separate referendums for greater control over their own affairs in 1997.

The British Isles have produced some of the world's greatest literature and have also been very influential in popular music. Popular sports first played in Britain include association football (soccer), rugby union, rugby league, cricket and lawn tennis.

A TOUTE HEURE

Steack au Poivre Feites 31F
Brokette de gigot Riz 33F
Cote à l'américaine 39F

▶ **What's on the menu?**
*Dishes of the day are chalked up on
the window of a Parisian restaurant.
Many people believe French food to be
the best in the world.*

MONACO

FRANCE

Dunkerque
Calais
Boulogne · Lille · BELGIUM
Montreuil · Arras · Douai · LUXEMBOURG
Valenciennes
Abbeville · Cambrai
Dieppe · St. Quentin · Hirson
Cherbourg · Fécamp · Amiens · Charleville-Mézières
Bay of · Bolbec · Montdidier
the Seine
Carentan · Le Havre · Rouen · Beauvais · Compiègne · Reims · Meuse · Verdun
St. Lô · Caen · Louviers · Seine · Marne
Gulf of St-Malo · Lisieux · Evreux · **Paris** · Meaux · Châlons-sur-Marne
Morlaix · Granville · Argentan · St. Germain-en-Laye · Versailles · St.Dizier · Toul
Brest · St-Malo · NORMANDY HILLS · Rambouillet · Seine
St-Brieuc · Dinan · Fontainebleau
Douarnenez · Fougeres · Alençon · Chartres · Nemours · Troyes
Quimper · Pontivy · Mayenne · Sens · Langres · LANGRES PLATEAU
Lorient · Rennes · Vitre · Laval · Orléans · Montargis · Auxerre · Dijon · S
Vannes · Le Mans · Gien
Redon · Loire · Blois · Auvallon · Dôle
St. Nazaire · Angers · Tours · Vierzon · Loire · Autun · Chalon-sur-S
Belle-Ile · Nantes · Saumur · Cher · Bourges · Nevers · Le Creusot
Châtellerault · Châteauroux · Montceau les Mines · St.Clau
La Roche-sur-Yon · Poiters · La Châtre · Moulins · Mâcon · Saône
Isle d'Yeu · Niort · Montluçon · Bourg-en-Bresse
Les Sables-d'Olonne · Civray · **FRANCE** · Vichy · Villefranches
Ré I. · La Rochelle · Limoges · Clermont-Ferrand · Lyon · Villeurban
Rochefort · Cognac · Angoulême · ▲Puy de Sancy · Loire · Vienne · Chambé
Oléron I. · Royan · Nontron · 1,888m · St.-Etienne · Annonay · Isère
Pauillac · Barbezieux · MASSIF · Romans-sur-Isère
Gironde · Périgueux · CENTRAL · Privas · Valence
Libourne · Bergerac · Souillac · Aurillac · Rhône
Bordeaux · Dordogne · Cère · Romans-sur-Isère · Montélimar
Marmande · Lot · Rodez · Lot · Mende · CEVENNES
LES · Cahors · Aveyron · Millau · Alès · Avignon · Carper
LANDES · Agen · Montauban · Tarn · Albi · Nîmes · Durance · Arles
Monte-de-Marsan · Gaillac · LANGUEDOC · Montpellier
Bayonne · Adour · Auch · Toulouse · Castres · Sète · Marseill
Biarritz · Garonne · Carcassonne · Béziers
Pau · Ariège · Aude · Narbonne
PYRENEES · Tarbes · Lourdes · St. Gaudens · Foix
SPAIN · Perpignan
ANDORRA

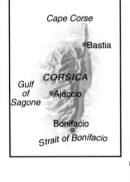

Cape Corse

·Bastia

CORSICA

Gulf
of
Sagone · ·Ajaccio

Bonifacio

Strait of Bonifacio

FRANCE
AND MONACO

Frรance is one of the larger countries of western Europe. It forms a bridge between the north and south of the continent, with coasts on the cool English Channel, the stormy Atlantic Ocean and the warm, blue Mediterranean Sea. Monaco is a tiny independent principality on its southern coast.

France is a beautiful country which lies at the heart of western Europe. Its climate is cool and temperate in the north, and warm and dry in the south. The population numbers about 58.6 million.

Western regions include the massive peaks of the Pyrenees, vineyards and pine forests, peaceful rivers and sandy shores along the Bay of Biscay. The north includes the stormy headlands of Brittany, the cliffs of Normandy and the Channel ports. Rolling fertile plains are drained by the winding River Seine, over whose banks and islands sprawls the French capital. Paris is one of the world's great cities, with broad avenues, historic palaces and churches and the famous landmark of the Eiffel Tower, a high iron pinnacle erected in 1889. The east of France is bordered by the wooded hills of

the Ardennes and the Vosges, which stretch southwards to the high forested slopes of the Jura mountains and finally the spectacular glaciers and ridges of the Alps. Mont Blanc is the highest peak in western Europe, at 4,807 metres above sea level.

The rocks of the Massif Central, shaped by ancient volcanoes, rise in central southern France, to the west of the Rhône valley. Here too are many famous vineyards. The sun-baked hills of southern France border the warm waters of the Mediterranean Sea. This coast includes the wetlands of the Camargue, famous for their wild horses and varied bird life, as well as the great seaport of Marseilles and the fashionable yachting marinas of Cannes. The sunny south coast and uplands make up a region known as Provence, which attracts many tourists. The Mediterranean island of Corsica, which lies to the southeast, is also ruled by France.

France has long played a major part in world history, from the Middle Ages onwards. During the reign of Louis XIV (1638-1715) it became the most powerful and influential country in Europe. The French Revolution of 1789 saw the violent overthrow of the king and the ruling classes. A general called Napoleon Bonaparte had himself crowned emperor in 1804 and conquered large areas of Europe, before being defeated by British and Prussian troops in 1815.

The French language is still spoken in those parts of the world which formerly made up France's large overseas empire, built up in the 1700s and 1800s. These include large areas of Africa, the Caribbean and the Québec province of Canada. French is spoken throughout France, although there are many strong dialects and several separate minority languages.

The French people are descended from a Celtic people called the Gauls and also

▲ *Château de Chaumont*
This is one of many fairytale castles and stately homes built in the valley of the River Loire. This picturesque region attracts many visitors to its fine scenery and beautiful cuisine.

◄ *Next stop, the Casino...*
Take a bus to the casino in Monte Carlo, and you may come back in a Rolls Royce! Fortunes are won and lost in the capital of Monaco.

◀ Market produce
Fresh produce is the key to good cooking. The French countryside produces apples, pears and cherries, and choice vegetables such as beans, peas, asparagus and artichokes.

from Germanic peoples such as the Franks and the Vikings (who settled in Normandy). Within France are several other peoples with their own languages and

THE WORLD'S FINEST WINES
Grape vines are trimmed at Saint Hippolyte, in Alsace. France has been producing wines since Roman times and its regions have given their name to many world-famous wines, such as Burgundy, Bordeaux and Champagne. Cognac makes the finest brandy – a strong spirit also made from grapes.

distinct cultures, such as the Bretons (another branch of Celts, who are closely related to the Cornish and Welsh of Great Britain), the Basques and the Catalans (whose homeland stretches into Spain), the Alsatians and the Corsicans. Algerians and other North African peoples have also settled in France. About 90 per cent of the population is Roman Catholic, with most of the remainder being Protestant Christians, Muslims or Jews.

Modern France, which suffered invasions by Germany during the World Wars of 1914-18 and 1939-45, is a republic. It has been working for European unity since the 1950s and is a key member of the European Union (EU). As a major industrial power it produces cars, aerospace equipment, chemicals and textiles. The country is also renowned for its wines, its cheeses, its fine cooking or haute cuisine and the great fashion houses of Paris. France has produced many of the world's greatest writers, painters, musicians, scientists and film-makers.

A section of the Mediterranean coast is occupied by a very small principality called Monaco. This has close links with its large neighbour and shares the same currency, the franc. Most of this state is taken up by the city of Monte Carlo, famous for its casino and the annual Monaco Grand Prix Formula 1 motor racing event.

Sylt
Flensburg
BALTIC SEA
Schleswig
Kiel Bay
NORTH SEA
Kiel
Fehmarn
Rügen
Helgoland
Rendsburg
Neumünster
Mecklenburg Bay
Stralsund
Lübeck
Rostock
Cuxhaven
Itzehoe
Wismar
Güstrow
Neubrandenburg
Elmshorn
Norderstedt
Schwerin
Wilhelmshaven
Bremerhaven
Hamburg
Müritz Lake
Neustrelitz
Emden
Buxtehude
Papenburg
Oldenburg
Bremen
Lüneburg
Eberswalde-Finow
Oder
Delmenhorst
Vechta
Nienburg
Celle
Stendal
Wittenberge
Nordhorn
Weser
Aller
Wolfsburg
Brandenburg
Berlin
Rheine
Osnabrück
Hannover
Wolfsburg
Potsdam
Frankfurt (an der Oder)
POLAND
Gronau
Bielefeld
Minden
Hildesheim
Brunswick (Braunschweig)
Magdeburg
Eisenhüttenstadt
Münster
TEUTOBURG FOREST
Hameln
Salzgitter
Bocholt
Holzminden
Bad Harzburg
Halberstadt
Dessau
Elbe
Cottbus
Dinslaken
Paderborn
Göttingen
Nordhausen
Halle
Hoyerswerda
Duisburg
Dortmund
Arnsberg
Kassel
Münden
Leipzig
Meissen
Krefeld
Essen
Wuppertal
GERMANY
Görlitz
Mönchen-Gladbach
Düsseldorf
Remscheid
Solingen
Mühlhausen
Weimar
Erfurt
Jena
Gera
Dresden
Freiberg
Aachen
Bonn
Siegen
Marburg
Alsfeld
THURINGIAN FOREST
Chemnitz
Zwickau
Neuwied
Giessen
Fulda
Suhl
Plauen
Daun
Koblenz
Werra
Main
Hof
Wiesbaden
Frankfurt am Main
Coburg
Mainz
Offenbach
Schweinfurt
Bayreuth
BOHEMIAN FOREST
CZECH REPUBLIC
Trier
Darmstadt
Würzburg
Bamberg
HUNSRÜCK
Worms
Kitzingen
STEIGERWALD
Ludwigshafen
Mannheim
Jagst
Fürth
Nuremberg (Nürnberg)
Kaiserslautern
Heidelberg
Saarbrücken
Heilbronn
Regensburg
Karlsruhe
Pforzheim
Baden-Baden
Stuttgart
Aalen
Ingolstadt
Passau
Tübingen
SWABIAN JURA
Danube
Krems
Reutlingen
Ulm
Augsburg
Braunau
Linz
Vie
Freiburg
BLACK FOREST
Memmingen
Lech
Munich (München)
Inn
Wels
Steyr
Danube
St Pölte
Schaffhausen
Konstanz
Kempten
Rosenheim
Salzach
Gmunden
Salzburg
B
Winterthur
Lake Constance (Bodensee)
Hallein
AUSTRIA
Basel
Baden
St Gallen
Zugspitze 2,963 m
Kufstein
Kitzbühel
NIEDERE TAUERN
Kapfen
Neuchâtel
Solothurn
Zurich
Zug
LIECHTENSTEIN
Innsbruck
HOHE TAUERN
Leoben
Lake Neuchâtel
Bern
Lucerne
Vaduz
Brenner
Grossglockner 2,863 m
Mur
Graz
Fribourg
Thun
SWITZERLAND
Chur
Davos
Wolfsberg
Lausanne
Interlaken
Andermatt
ITALY
Klagenfurt
Lake Geneva
Montreux
BERNESE ALPS
LEPONTINE ALPS
St Moritz
Villach
Drava
Geneva
Thonon
Zermatt
Locarno
Bellinzona
SLOVENIA
Martigny
Matterhorn 4,478 m
Monte Rosa 4,634 m
Lugano

GERMANY

AUSTRIA

SWITZERLAND

LIECHTENSTEIN

BELGIUM

LUXEMBOURG

FRANCE

GERMANY
AND THE ALPS

Germany extends southwards from the windy coasts of the North Sea and the Baltic to the snowy peaks of the Alps, in the southern region of Bavaria (Bayern). The Alps form the biggest mountain chain of Western Europe and are taken up by three other countries – Switzerland, Austria and tiny Liechtenstein.

Germany lies between Western and Central Europe. Its western regions, or Länder, take in the Black Forest and the Rivers Rhine and Moselle, which wind through steep valleys planted with vines. Its eastern Länders flank the Bohemian Forest, the Ore Mountains (Erzgerbirge) and the Rivers Oder and Neisse.

▲ **Dream castle for a mad king**
Romantic Neuschwanstein Castle was built in the 1870s for the mad King Ludwig II of Bavaria.

Germany's northern coasts are made up of sand dunes and offshore islands. The Baltic and North Sea sections are linked by the busy waterway of the Kiel Canal. Northern Germany is flat, mainly crossed by great rivers such as the Elbe and Weser. Major ports include Bremen, Hamburg, Lübeck and Rostock.

The northwest includes the industrial belt around the Ruhr river, which flows into the Rhine at Duisburg. The northeast takes up part of a great plain which stretches eastwards into Poland and Russia. On its edge, set amongst forests and lakes, is the capital city of Berlin.

In central Germany, the landscape rises from sandy heaths and moors to the highlands of the Harz mountains. Two great rivers, the Main and the Danube, cross the southern half of the country, which rises towards the high peaks of the Bavarian Alps. Germany has many large, modern industrial or commercial cities, such as Frankfurt-am-Main and Stuttgart, as well as pretty villages,

▲ *Fine wines*
Perfect soil and weather conditions in the Rhine valley make wine production a huge industry in Germany.

cathedrals and ruined castles dating back to the Middle Ages.

For most of its history Germany has been divided into different states. In the Middle Ages the country was a patchwork of small nations and cities. Many of them were part of a federation called the Holy Roman Empire. In the 1700s the northeastern kingdom of Prussia became the most powerful of the German states.

Germany united as a single empire in 1870, but it was disastrously defeated in the First World War (1914-18). A dictator called Adolf Hitler, leader of the racist Nazi Party, came to power in the 1930s. During the Second Word War (1939-45) he ordered the invasion of most of Europe as well as the murder of millions of Jews, Gypsies and political opponents in death camps.

Defeated again, Germany and the city of Berlin was divided into two, between the communist east and the capitalist west.

It was 1990 before Germany was reunited. Germany today is a federal republic, with considerable powers devolved to the Länder. It is a leading member of the European Union and is a major world producer of cars, electrical and household goods, medicines and chemicals.

Despite its troubled history, Germany has been home to many of Europe's greatest thinkers, writers, artists and musical composers – Johann Wolfgang von Goethe was born in Frankfurt-am-Main in 1749 and

TASTY FARE
Germany is famous for its wines and its beers, and is said to produce over 1,500 different kinds of sausage. Bread is made from rye as well as wheat and popular dishes include veal and pork. The most famous Swiss dish is fondue, Gruyère or Emmentaler cheese melted in a pot with white wine, kirsch, pepper and garlic. Forks of bread are dipped into the sauce. Vienna, the Austrian capital is famous for delicious tarts and cakes served with coffee and cream.

▲ *Swiss chalets, snowy peaks*
Traditional 'chalets', timber houses with broad roofs, may be seen in the villages around Lake Thun, in Switzerland.

Ludwig van Beethoven in Bonn in 1770.

Switzerland is a small, wealthy country set amongst the lakes and snowy peaks of the Alps and the Jura ranges. Its beautiful landscape and historical towns attract many tourists. In all the Alpine countries there are pretty villages of wooden houses built with wide, sloping roofs designed to withstand the heavy winter snowfall. Swiss industries include dairy produce, precision instruments and finance. Zurich is a world centre of banking, while Geneva is the headquarters of many international agencies, such as the Red Cross and the World Health Organization.

To the east, the tiny country of Liechtenstein is closely linked with Switzerland and uses the same currency. The land of Austria descends from the soaring peaks of the Alps to the flat lands of the Danube river valley. Austria once ruled a large empire which stretched eastwards into Hungary and southwards into Italy. Today Austria still plays an important part in Europe, making its living from tourism, farming, forestry and manufacture. Austria too has a rich background in music and the arts.

German is spoken through most of the region, with a great variety of dialects. In German cities you may also hear Turkish and southern European languages being spoken, as people from other countries have come to seek work in Germany since the 1960s. In parts of Switzerland there are also speakers of French, Italian and Romansh. Northern Germany and Switzerland are mostly Protestant, while southern Germany and Austria are mostly Roman Catholic.

▼ *Watching the world go by*
Cafés, shops and hotels line the longest street in west Berlin. This is the smart Kurfürstendamm, known for short as the 'Ku'damm'.

◄ *East Berlin, reunited with the west*
The River Spree flows into east Berlin near the avenue of Unter den Linden. From 1961 until 1989 the city of Berlin was divided by a wall manned by armed guards.

ANDORRA

Bay of Biscay

Cape Peñas

El Ferrol

Cape
Finisterre

Carballo   Villalba

Oviedo   Gijón
Llanes   Santander   San Sebastián   FRAN

CANTABRIAN   MOUNTAINS   Bilbao

Lugo   Fonsagrada

Santiago de Compostela

Sarria

Reinosa   Vitoria   Pamplona   PYRENEES

Ebro   Arga   Pico de
                                        3.40

Lalin

Vigo   Miño   Orense   SIERRA CABRERA   León   Astorga   Osorno   Burgos   Logroño

Gállego

Cinca

Monforte de Lemos

Sil

Villada   Palencia   Soria   Ebro   Saragossa

Braga   Baltar   La Gudina

Esla

Mogadouro   Bragança   Bruti   Brenti

Vila Real

Zamora   Valladolid   Duero   Jalón   Caspe

S P A I N

Porto   Lamego   Douro

Medina del Campo   Tormes   Segovia   SIERRA DE GUADARRAMA   Tortosa

PORTUGAL

Salamanca   Avila   Guadalajara   Tajuña   Tajo   Morella   Vina

Aviero   Viseu   Cuidad Rodrigo   Alcalá de Henares   Teruel   Castellón de la Plana   Costa del A

Guarda   Bejar   Madrid   Cuenca

Coimbra   Covilhã   SIERRA DE GREDOS   Aranjuez   Turia   Sagunto

Castelo Branco   Plasencia   Tajo   Mijares

Leiria   Toledo   Requena   Valencia

Tomar   Tagus   Cáceres   Trujillo   MONTES DE TOLEDO   Júcar   Gulf o Valen

Caldas da Rainha   Portalegre   Villarrobledo   Alcira

Santarém   Daimiel   Albacete   Alcoy

Lisbon   Badajoz   Don Benito   Manzanares   Almansa   Alicante

Almendralejo   Guadiana   Ciudad Real   Alcaraz   Yecla   Elche

Setúbal   Évora   Valdepeñas   Orihuela   Costa Blanca

Ardila   Puertollano   SIERRA DE SEGURA   Murcia

Pozoblanco   Segura

Beja   Azuaga   SIERRA MORENA   La Carolina   Moratalla   Lorca   Cartagena   Cape Palos

Guadiana   Linares   Cehegín   Aguilas

Constantina   Córdoba   Jaén   Baza   Huércal Overa

Chanca   Nerva   Guadalquivir   Martos   Guadix

Lagos   Huelva   Seville   Puente Genil   Granada   Almería   Costa Blanca

Faro   Costa de la Luz   Osuna   Genil   Mulhacén 3,478m

Cape Saint Vincent   Algarve   Gulf of Cadiz   Morón de la Frontera   Antequera   SIERRA NEVADA   Berja   Cape Gata

Jerez de la Frontera   Ronda   Málaga   Motril   Costa del Sol   M E D I T E R R A N E A N   S E A

Cádiz   SIERRA DE RONDA   Marbella

Gibraltar (U.K.)

Algeciras   Strait of Gibraltar

Cueta (Spain)

PORTUGAL

Melilla (Spain)

SPAIN

THE IBERIAN PENINSULA

The Iberian peninsula is in southwestern Europe, jutting out like a great fist into the Atlantic Ocean. It is bordered to the north by the stormy Bay of Biscay and to the south by the Mediterranean Sea and the Balearic Islands. The region is occupied by Spain, Portugal, Andorra and Gibraltar.

The Iberian Peninsula's north coast, green from high rainfall, rises to the Cantabrian mountains, while the snowy Pyrenees form a high barrier along the Spanish-French frontier. These mountains are the location of a tiny independent country called Andorra. Another snow-capped range, the Sierra Nevada, runs parallel with the peninsula's southern coast.

▶ A corner of old Seville
Seville is a beautiful old city in the Anadalucía region of Spain. The bell tower of its massive cathedral was once part of a Muslim mosque.

◀ Earthenware pots
Containers made of terracotta can be seen all over the Mediterranean. These traditional designs are centuries old.

The Spanish capital, Madrid, lies right at the centre of the Iberian peninsula. Much of this inland region is taken up by an extremely dry, rocky plateau, the Meseta, which swelters in the heat of summer. Spain's southern coast sweeps down to the Strait of Gibraltar, just 13 kilometres from the mainland of Africa. The steep rock of Gibraltar, controlling the entrance to the Mediterranean Sea, is a British colony. The west of the Iberian peninsula takes in rocky, forested highlands and the fertile plains of Portugal, crossed by great rivers. Lisbon, the Portuguese capital, lies on the north shore of the River Tagus.

Spain and Portugal are the two largest Iberian countries. Both have a rich history. They were conquered in the early Middle Ages by the Moors – Muslim Berbers and Arabs from North Africa, who left behind fine palaces and cities. Eventually the peninsula was reconquered by

▲ *In the highlands of Portugal*
Vineyards cover the sunny slopes of Buçaco, to the north of Coimbra. Portugal produces many red and rosé wines.

Christians from the north. Portugal and Spain led the European exploration of Africa and Asia, and went on to discover the 'New World' of the Americas in the 1490s and 1500s. Spanish and Portuguese are still the chief languages of Central and South America. Both Spain and Portugal suffered rule by dictators for much of the twentieth century, but today both are democracies and members of the European Union.

Spain produces olives, citrus fruits, wines and sherries, and has a large fishing fleet. It has reserves of iron ore and produces steel and motor vehicles. Portugal is one of western Europe's poorer countries. It produces wine and port, a strong sweet wine which

▼ *Along the Costa del Sol*
Spain's Costa del Sol ('sunshine coast') is in the south. Nerja, a former fishing village, attracts many tourists.

takes its name from the city of Oporto. Fishing villages line the Atlantic coast and cork is cut from the thick bark of a kind of oak tree.

Many tourists visit the Iberian peninsula, enjoying the small whitewashed villages, the historical towns, the great cathedrals and the medieval castles. The warm beaches of the south, lined by high-rise hotels, are especially popular with holiday-makers from northern Europe.

The whole region is strongly Roman Catholic, and life in both Spain and Portugal is marked by colourful festivals marking saints' days.

▲ *From the days of the Moors*
The fabulous Mezquita in Córdoba, Spain, is a mosque from the Middle Ages, when the Muslim city was a great centre of civilization.

◀ *Paella delight*
The best known Spanish dish is paella. Cooked in a heavy pan, it includes saffron rice, chicken or seafood, as well as garlic and vegetables.

During Holy Week, the period before the Christian festival of Easter, holy statues are carried through the streets.

Spain is famous for flamenco, a fiery combination of Gypsy guitar, wild singing and strutting, stamping dance steps. Portugal has fado, a sadder, more plaintive style of folk song. Bullfighting is an ancient Spanish tradition, full of colourful ceremony but criticized as cruel by many foreign visitors.

IBERIAN PEOPLES

The Iberian peninsula is home to many different peoples, cultures and languages and this has led to conflict in some regions.

The Basques live in the far north and their homeland stretches westwards from the city of Bilbao into France. Their language, Euskara, is not related to any other and may be the oldest in Europe.

The Galicians live along the rías or sea inlets of the northwest and they claim descent from the ancient Celts. Their language is called Gallego.

The Catalans live in the regions around the great cultural centre of Barcelona, as well as in Andorra and across the border in France. The Catalan language is widely spoken.

SWITZERLAND

AUSTRIA

SLOVENIA

Mont Blanc 4,807m

Monte Rosa 4,634m

L. Maggiore

L. Como

Bolzano

Trento

Borgo

Udine

Trieste

Lecco

Bergamo

Treviso

Piave

Biella

Monza

Verona

Vicenza

Portogruaro

Milan

Brescia

L. Garda

Venice

Ticino

Lodi

Padua

Turin

Pavia

Cremona

Mantova

Chioggia

Oglio

Po

Adria

Alessandra

Piacenza

Parma

Panaro

Ferrara

Comacchio

Tanaro

Carpi

Reggio nell'Emilia

Modena

Reno

Ravenna

Novi Ligure

Bologna

Rimini

Cuneo

Savona

Genoa

Forlì

Pesaro

FRANCE

Gulf of Genoa

La Spezia

Carrara

San Marino

SAN MARINO

Ancona

MONACO

LIGURIAN SEA

Massa

Viareggio

Lucca

Pistoia

Arno

ITALY

Pisa

Florence

Iesi

Livorno

Siena

Arezzo

Gubbio

Macerata

Capraia

Cortona

Perugia

San Benedetto

Elba

Piombino

L. Trasimeno

I T A L Y

Teramo

Grosseto

Terni

Giglio

L. Bolsena

Corno Grande 2,912m

Pescara

Corsica (France)

Civitavecchia

Vasto

Vatican City (in Rome)

Avezzano

Termoli

L. V

Rome

Agnone

Latina

Isernia

Fogg

Benevento

Gulf of Gaeta

Naples

Asinara

Gulf of Asinara

Strait of Bonifacio

Olbia

VATICAN CITY

Vesuvius 1,227m

Ischia

Salerno

Alghero

Sassari

Gulf of Naples

Capri

Tirso

Nuoro

Gulf of Orosei

San Pietro

S a r d i n i a

Oristano

Cagliari

Gulf of Cagliari

MALTA

Strom

Salina

Lipari

LIPARI ISLANDS

Vulcano

Cape San Vito

Palermo

Messina

Trapani

Alcamo

S i c i l y

Mt. Et

Mazara del Vallo

Catania

G of C

Agrigento

Caltanissetta

Pantelleria

Gulf of Gela

Syracuse

Ragusa

M A L T A   C H A N

MALTA

ITALY

ITALY AND ITS NEIGHBOURS

Italy occupies a long peninsula in the Mediterranean Sea. It takes in the large islands of Sardinia and Sicily and also surrounds two patches of independent territory, Vatican City and San Marino. Malta is an island nation lying to the south.

Shaped like a high-heeled boot, Italy divides the blue waters of the Mediterranean into the Ligurian and Tyrrhenian Seas in the west and the Adriatic Sea in the east.

The north of Italy descends from the high, snowy peaks and sparkling lakes of the Alps to wide, fertile plains around the River Po. The wealthiest industrial cities, such as Milan and Bologna, are located in the north.

A long chain of mountains, the Appenines, run down the spine of Italy and takes in the little state of San Marino. The mountains are wooded and a home to a rich vaiety of wildlife, including rare grey wolves. The mountains are flanked by the vineyards of

▲ *Streets made of water*
A maze of canals serve as streets in Venice, one of Europe's most beautiful cities. Boats are the mode of transport.

Tuscany and the rich farmland around the Bay of Naples. In the far south are hot, dry plains, rocks and scrub. This is the poorest part of Italy. Southern Italy and its islands form one of the world's danger zones for earthquakes. Famously violent volcanoes

◀ On the Gulf of Salerno
The pretty town of Positano climbs steeply from blue seas. Tourist resorts in this region also include Amalfi and the island of Capri.

world. Factories produce cars, textiles and leather goods. Milan is famous for fashion, and Venice for glass-making.

Modern Italy has only been united since 1861, but in ancient times Rome was the capital of a vast empire which stretched across western Europe, southwest Asia and North Africa. During the 1400s and 1500s cities such as Florence saw a great flowering of scholarship and the arts, known as the Renaissance ('rebirth'). Few other countries can boast so many well-preserved historical buildings and works of art. Tourists from all over the world visit Italy to see its ancient sites.

Italian, based on the ancient Latin language, is spoken throughout Italy,

include Vesuvius, near Naples, and Etna, on Sicily.

The Italian capital is the ancient city of Rome, on the River Tiber. One district of Rome, Vatican City, is the world's smallest independent state, serving as headquarters for the Roman Catholic Church and its Popes.

Italy was a founder member of what is now the European Union. Olives and grapes grow well in its sunny climate and Italy is the largest wine producer in the

◀ St Peter's Square
This part of Vatican City, in the centre of Rome, is where crowds of Christians often gather to be blessed by the Pope.

▶ The Leaning Tower of Pisa
This medieval bell tower may be seen in Pisa. Built on unstable ground, it now leans over from the vertical by about 5 metres.

but in border regions you may hear other languages, such as French, German or Slovenian. The Ladin language is spoken in the Dolomite mountains of the northeast, and the people of Sardinia speak their own ancient dialect of Italian.

Italians are nearly all Roman Catholics. Many are great lovers of opera and cinema and supporters of football. The population as a whole numbers about 57.4 million. In the last 150 years many Italians have left their homeland in search of work overseas, and there are large Italian communities in Northern Europe, the United States of America and Australia.

To the south of Sicily, towards the coast of North Africa, is the chain of islands which make up Malta. Its capital is the seaport of Valletta. Malta was a British colony from 1814 until 1964, when it became independent. The population of over 360,000 lives on the islands of Malta, Gozo and Comino. The Maltese have their own language, which has been influenced by dialects of Italian and Arabic. The chief industries are tourism, ship building and repair.

▲ *Spaghetti Bolognese*
Spaghetti is a kind of pasta. Here it is served with a meat and tomato sauce, invented in the city of Bologna.

◀ *Into the Grand Canal*
The Customs House, built in 1672, dominates this section of Venice's Grand Canal. Many artists have painted this scene over the centuries.

ESTONIA

▲ **Traditional sounds**
The zither is a flat,
stringed instrument which
has been played by folk
musicians in Central
Europe for centuries.

LITHUANIA

ESTONIA
Tallinn
Kohtla-Järve
Hiiumaa
Lake Peipus
Saaremaa
Pärnu
Tartu
RUSSIA
Gulf of Riga
Munamagi 318 m ▲
Ventspils
LATVIA
Jurmala
Gaizina 311 m ▲
Saldus
Riga
Liepāja
Jelgava
Siauliai
Daugavpils
Panevezys
Utena
Klaipeda
LITHUANIA
Ukmerge
Nemunas (Neman)
Kaunas
Vilnius
Kaliningrad (RUSSIA)
311 m ▲
Gulf of Gdansk
Gdynia
Kaliningrad
BELARUS
Gdansk
Kolobrzeg
Elblag
Olsztyn
N O R T H   E U R O P E A N   P L A I N
Szczecin
Bydgoscz
Bialystock
Gorzow Wielkopolski
Torun
Poznan
Plock
LATVIA
Kalisz
Warsaw
P O L A N D
Glogow
Lodz
GERMANY
Odra (Oder)
Radom
Lublin
Wroclaw
Kielce
Chelm
Walbrzych
Czestochowa
POLAND
SUDETES MOUNTAINS
Bytom
Karlovy Vary
Prague
Katowice
Krakow
UKRAINE
Plzen
Pardubice
Tychy
Tarnow
Rzeszow
Bielsko-Biala
CZECH REPUBLIC
Ostrava
CARPATHIAN MOUNTAINS
BOHEMIA
Olomouc
BOHEMIA
MORAVIA
Zilina
Presov
Cesky Budejovice
Brno
Rysy Peak 2,499m ▲
AUSTRIA
Trencin
Kosice
SLOVAK REPUBLIC
Nytra
Miskolc
SLOVAKIA
Bratislava
Mt. Kekes ▲1,015m
Debrecen
Danube
Györ
Budapest
CZECH REPUBLIC
Tatabanya
Koros
Szombathely
HUNGARY
Bekescsaba
ROMANIA
Lake Balaton
Tisza
Kaposvar
Szeged
Pécs
CROATIA
YUGOSLAVIA
HUNGARY

CENTRAL EUROPE

Three small countries cluster around the eastern shores of the Baltic Sea – Estonia, Latvia and Lithuania. Poland lies on the Baltic's southern shore, between Germany and Eastern Europe. Across the mountains of southern Poland lie the Czech and Slovak Republics and Hungary, on the River Danube.

The Baltic states of Estonia, Latvia and Lithuania are made up of forests and lakes, farmland and industrial cities. For much of their history they have been ruled by their larger neighbours, and were part of the Soviet Union (today's Russian Federation) from

▲ *Dolls in the market*
Sets of wooden dolls which fit one into the other, in the Russian style, are popular tourist souvenirs.

◄ **The last of the bisons**
The European bison, or wisent, was rescued from the brink of extinction in the 1950s and can be seen today in Poland's Bialowieza forest.

▼ **Tasty exports**
Barrels at the brewery waiting for export. The Czech republic produces beers which are now on sale throughout the world.

1940 until 1991. During this period many Russians settled in the region. However, each of the Baltic states managed to keep its own language and culture.

Poland is a large country which has also known invasions and foreign rule through much of its history. Like the countries to the south, Poland remained under strict Soviet influence from the late 1940s until 1989. The Poles, a Slavic people, also kept alive a pride in their country's traditions.

The lands near Poland's Baltic coast are dotted with lakes. The north of the country is flat, forested land,

part of the great plain which stretches from eastern Germany into Russia. It is cold and snowy in winter, but warm in summer. In southern Poland the land rises to highlands and the jagged peaks of the Tatra mountains. Poland has reserves of coal and produces steel and heavy machinery. Its farmlands produce wheat, potatoes and beet. Its most famous export is vodka, a fiery alcoholic spirit.

Slovakia and the Czech Republic were a single country until 1993. Slovakia is a land of high mountains dropping to fertile farmland around the River Danube, which forms its southeastern border. When the two countries divided, most of the industries lay on the Czech side of the border. The Czech Republic, with its capital at Prague, produces beer, glass, ceramics, steel and machinery. The country

▲ *Old-time Prague*
This old clock may be seen in Prague, capital of the Czech Republic. This fine city on the River Vltava attracts many tourists.

▶ *Waterchess in the baths*
Here is the perfect way to enjoy the beneficial spa waters which are a normal part of Hungarian life.

SOUNDS OF CENTRAL EUROPE

The balalaika is a musical instrument with a triangular body and a long neck like a guitar. Its jangling sounds are popular in Central Europe, Russia and the Balkans. The folk music of the region also makes use of fiddles. It has been influenced in places by Gypsy dance music and has in turn influenced some classical composers.

▶ *Soldiers on Parade*
Lithuanian troops march past during the Independence Day celebrations. Lithuania finally won full independence in 1991.

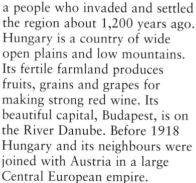

is bordered by mountains and, in the east, by the Bohemian Forest. Bohemia was the name of the kingdom that grew up here in the Middle Ages.

The Czechs and Slovaks are both Slavic peoples, but the Hungarians are Magyars, a people who invaded and settled the region about 1,200 years ago. Hungary is a country of wide open plains and low mountains. Its fertile farmland produces fruits, grains and grapes for making strong red wine. Its beautiful capital, Budapest, is on the River Danube. Before 1918 Hungary and its neighbours were joined with Austria in a large Central European empire.

Central Europe has also been settled by other peoples over the ages, including the Roma (Gypsies) and the Jews. Central Europe is largely Roman Catholic in faith, with Protestant and Russian Orthodox groups around the Baltic.

◀ *Five horsepower*
This skilled horseman controls five lively horses at a Herdsman and Horseman Show in Kiskunsagi National Park, Hungary.

EUROPE

ROMANIA

BULGARIA

SLOVENIA

CROATIA

UKRAINE

Satu Mare
Bala Mare
Botosani
MOLDOVA
Iasi
Oradea
Cluj-Napoca
Bacau
AUSTRIA
Maribor
Tirgu Mures
Siret
Triglav 2,863 m
Ljubljana
Sava
Koprivnica
HUNGARY
Arad
Mures
Alba Iulia
ROMANIA
Galati
SLOVENIA
Zagreb
Subotica
Timisoara
Deva
Sibiu
Brasov
Braila
Rijeka
Kupa
CROATIA
Drava
Osijek
VOJVODINA
Resita
Moldoveanu 2,543 m
TRANSYLVANIAN ALPS
Jiu
Pula
Bihac
Prijedor
Novi Sad
Belgrade
Ploiesti
DOBRUJA
Cres
Gospic
Banja Luka
Brcko
Pitesti
Losinj
BOSNIA - HERZEGOVINA
Tuzla
Sabac
Smederevo
Craiova
Bucharest
Zadar
Zenica
Valjevo
Negotin
Constanta
Dugi I.
Livno
Sarajevo
Srebrenica
Kragujevac
Vidin
Dunarea (Danube)
Ruse
Dobrich
Sibenik
Split
Mostar
Krusevac
Nis
Mikhaylovgrad
Pleven
Lovech
Turgovishte
Kamchiya
Varna
Vis
Korcula
Novi Pazar
SERBIA
Leskovac
Sofia
Kazanluk
Sliven
Burgas
Lastovo
Mljet
Dubrovnik
YUGOSLAVIA
MONTENEGRO
Pristina
BULGARIA
Jundzha
Yambol
Podgorica
Pec
KOSOVO
Urosevac
Pernik
Musala Peak 2,925 m
Pasardzhik
Stara Zagora
Shkoder
Lake Scutari
Skopje
Plovdiv
Khaskovo
Drin Gulf
Mt Korabit 2,751 m
Tetovo
MACEDONIA
Struma
RHODOPE MOUNTAINS
Smolyan
Orestiás
Durrës
Tirane
Prilep
Palikastron
Drama
Komotini
Elbasan
Lake Ohrid
Bitola
Kilkis
Serrai
Xánthi
Alexandroúpolis
Lake Prespa
Edhessa
Kavalla
Thásos
ALBANIA
Naousa
Thessaloniki
Samothrace
Vlora
Ptolemais
Alakmon
Limnos
Gjirokaster
Mt Olympus 2,917 m
Mt Athos 2,033 m
GREECE
Ioánnina
Trikkala
Lárisa
Kérkira
Corfu
Párga
Vólos
Skiathos
Lesbos
Mitilíni
Arta
Kardhitsa
Skópelos
Skíros
Pálairos
Lamia
Euboea
AEGEAN
Leukas
Parnassus 2,547 m
Kími
SEA
Chios
Astakós
Agrínion
Khalkis
Cephalonia
Ithaca
Pátrai
Mégara
Marathon
Ándros
Sámos
IONIAN SEA
Amaliás
Lambia
Corinth
Piraeus
Athens
Ikaría
Zante
Pírgos
Alfios
Argos
Láyrion
Kéa
Kíthnos
Mikonos
Pátmos
Tripolis
Návplion
Galatás
Síros
Páros
Náxos
Léros
PELOPONNESUS
Sérifos
Kálimnos
Kalamáta
Sparta
Sífnos
Cos
Areópolis
Mílos
Íos
Astipálaia
Tílos
Neápolis
Thíra
Rhodes
Cythera
Rhodes
Líndos
SEA OF CRETE
Kárpathos
Khaniá
Réthimnon
Tráklion
Mt. Ida 2,456 m
Crete

BOSNIA-HERZEGOVINA

ALBANIA

GREECE

MACEDONIA

THE BALKANS

The states of southern Central Europe are known as the Balkans. They take their name from the Balkan peninsula, a broad wedge of land which stretches south into the Mediterranean Sea. The Balkans include Romania, Bulgaria, Albania, Greece and the lands formerly grouped together as Yugoslavia.

The warm, blue waters around the Balkan coast form the Adriatic, Ionian, Aegean and Black Seas. The region is largely mountainous, with hot, dry summers. Winters are severe in the north of the region, but generally mild in the south. Violent earthquakes are common.

The Balkan countries produce fruit, wines and spirits, wheat, dairy products such as yoghurt and cheese, olives, sunflowers and tobacco.

▼ *Agricultural worker, Romania*
This lady wears the traditional headwear of scarf and straw hat to protect her from all weathers as she works on the land.

Many parts of the region are poor. All have experienced long centuries of war, invasion and occupation. Peoples of the Balkans include Southern Slavs (such as Serbs, Croats, Slovenes and Montenegrins), Albanians, Greeks, Bulgars, Turks, Roma (Gypsies) and Romanians. Religions include both Roman Catholic and Eastern Orthodox Christianity as well as Islam.

The northwest of the region is a patchwork of these peoples, each with their distinctive cultures, languages and beliefs. In the 1990s it exploded into bitter fighting and racial violence as the large nation of Yugoslavia broke up into separate

▼ *Pulled by oxen*
In the village of Szeg these Romanian farmers still use oxen to pull their hay wagons at harvest time.

independent states. These took the names of Slovenia, Croatia, Yugoslavia (Serbia and Montenegro), and Macedonia (which is also the name of the northernmost province of Greece). The tourist industry along the northern Adriatic coast came to an end.

From 1946 until 1985 the small country of Albania, with its capital at Tiranë, was led by a communist called Enver Hoxha. He kept the country isolated from the rest of Europe. After Hoxha's death Albania moved away from communist government. It suffered great poverty and in the 1990s collapsed into political unrest and civil war.

The northeast of the Balkan peninsula is occupied by Bulgaria, a land of fertile farmland to the south of the River Danube,

crossed by the Balkan and Rhodope mountain chains. Its northern neighbour is Romania, lying around the forested Carpathian mountain range and the Transylvanian Alps. On the Black Sea coast, the River Danube splits into separate waterways and forms a marshy delta region. The recent history of Romania has included the violent overthrow of the government in 1989.

The Balkan peninsula narrows to the south. Greece occupies the southern part of the mainland, which breaks up into the large headland of the Peloponnese and many scattered island chains. The largest island, mountainous Crete,

◀ *Croatian costume*
These folk musicians at Vrobovec in Croatia wear traditional costume. Croatian independence was recognized by the European Union in 1992.

◀ *Walking home after church*
These families are walking home after church, at Szeg in Romania. Most Romanians follow the Romanian Orthodox faith. Other Christian worshippers include Protestants, Uniates (Greek Catholics) and Roman Catholics.

◄ *The islands of Greece*
Thíra, also known as Santorini, is a popular tourist island to the north of Crete. Over 3,600 years ago it was the site of a massive volcanic eruption.

▼ *The Corinth Canal*
In 1893 the narrow strip of land joining the Peloponnese to the Greek mainland near Corinth was severed by a sheer, deep shipping canal.

marks the southern limits of Greek territory. Greece has many small, whitewashed villages and beautiful beaches which attract visitors from all over the world. It also has large industrial centres and seaports. Greece is a member of the European Union. Although many of its people are still poor farmers and fishermen, in recent years tourism has helped Greece to become wealthier than the other Balkan countries. There are large Greek-speaking communities overseas, especially in Cyprus, the United States and Australia.

WHO ARE THE BULGARIANS?
In Bulgaria, the traditional costume may still be worn for regional festivals or for folk dancing. Heritage and tradition are being emphasised in a bid to attract tourists. Bulgarian culture has many influences, from Ancient Thracian to Macedonian, Slavic, Bulgar, Turkish and Roma (Gypsy).

Greece was the centre of Europe's first great civilizations, between 4,000 and 2,000 years ago. It was here that democracy – meaning 'rule by the people' was first tried out. The ancient rock of the Acropolis, with its splendid temple, the Parthenon, still towers above the Greek capital, Athens. The ancient Greeks were great thinkers, poets, dramatists, sculptors and warriors. Under Alexander the Great (356-323BC) they conquered lands from Egypt to India, but were eventually defeated by the Romans.

RUSSIA AND ITS NEIGHBOURS

BELARUS

RUSSIA

UKRAINE

ARMENIA

GEORGIA

MOLDOVA

UZBEKISTAN

AZERBAIJAN

TAJIKSTAN

KYRGYZSTAN

TURKMENISTAN

KAZAKHSTAN

RUSSIA AND ITS NEIGHBOURS

The Russian Federation is the biggest country in the world, stretching from eastern Europe right across Asia to the Pacific Ocean. Around it are a number of smaller countries. Belarus, Ukraine and Moldova lie to the west. Georgia, Armenia and Azerbaijan lie to the southwest. Due south are the Central Asian states of Turkmenistan, Uzbekistan and Kazakhstan.

For most of the last 100 years this region was dominated by one huge country, called the USSR or Soviet Union. That nation was formed in the years after November 1917, when communist revolutionaries ('Bolsheviks') seized power from the emperors, or tsars, who had ruled Russia since the 1500s.

Communist rule ended in 1991 and many of the regions around the former Soviet borders then broke away to become independent countries – although most remained allies within a grouping called the Commonwealth of Independent States (CIS).

The remaining part of the former Soviet Union was renamed the 'Russian Federation'. The term 'Russia' really only refers to one part of that federation, but is often used as a short form for the whole country. In the 1990s there was conflict when other parts of the federation, such as Chechnya, tried to break away.

The Russian Federation is still by far the largest country in the world, stretching across two continents and eight time zones. A journey from Moscow to the Pacific coast, on the famous Trans-Siberian Railway, takes seven days.

The Russian capital is Moscow, a sprawling city of about 9

▼ *Siberian farmer*
This farmer works in extreme conditions. Winters in Siberia are severe with temperatures falling as low as -70°C (-94°F).

◄ The Moscow metro
Travellers crowd on to a Moscow underground railway station. The capital's Metro, built in the early days of communism, is decorated in a grand old-fashioned style.

million people. At its centre is the wide open space of Red Square and the walls of the Kremlin. This ancient fortress, which became the centre of government power in the old Soviet Union, contains fine old churches with gleaming domes. To the north is the former capital of St Petersburg, a splendid city founded by a tsar called Peter the Great in 1703.

Northern Russia is a land of tundra, where deep-frozen soil borders the Arctic Ocean. To the south is the great belt of forest known as taiga, whose spruce

trees are heavy with snow during the long, bitter winters. However, summers can be warm and sunny. To the south are the steppe grasslands, the shores of the Black Sea and the high mountains of the Caucasus. The Ural range, running from north to south, marks the border between European and Asian Russia.

Russia is rich in minerals and timber. Its industries were developed in a hurry during the Soviet years, but at great cost to the Russian people and the environment. Russia is still an economic giant, producing machinery, textiles, chemicals and vehicles and it still launches spacecraft. However, recent years have seen huge economic problems, rising crime and political unrest.

▼ Market stalls in Yerevan
Local produce is laid out at an indoor market in Yerevan. The countryside around the Armenian capital produces citrus fruits, grapes, figs, olives and almonds.

▼ A federation of peoples
Over 150 different peoples live in the Russian Federation, many with their own languages, traditions and costumes, still worn for special festivals or folk dances.

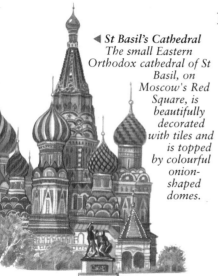

◀ St Basil's Cathedral The small Eastern Orthodox cathedral of St Basil, on Moscow's Red Square, is beautifully decorated with tiles and is topped by colourful onion-shaped domes.

Eighty per cent of the Russian Federation's population of 147,300,000 are Russians (a Slavic people), but the rest belong to many other ethnic groups which also live in the country. The Eastern Orthodox Church, no friend of the Bolsheviks, has today regained some of the power it enjoyed under the tsars.

Popular sports in Russia include football, ice hockey, athletics and ice skating. Russia has produced many of the greatest musical composers in history, such as Piotr Ilyich Tchaikovsky (1840-93), as well as wonderful ballet companies such as the Bolshoi and Kirov. Famous Russian writers include Leo Tolstoy, who wrote *War and Peace* in 1863-69.

Since independence, some of the other CIS countries have shared many of the same problems as Russia, including civil war, political unrest and organized crime. The western CIS lands are industrialized, with the rich black soil of the Ukrainian steppes providing a large yield of wheat. In the Caucasus region, sunny Georgia and Armenia grow citrus fruits and grapes.

The lands around the Caspian and Aral Seas include dusty, thin grasslands grazed by sheep and goats, mountains and deserts. Crops include cotton and wheat. Carpet-making is a traditional craft skill of the region. There are large reserves of oil and natural gas, which will have a great impact on the region's economy and development in the twenty-first century.

The western CIS countries, home to Slavs, Georgians and Armenians, have a long Christian tradition, but the Turkic and Mongol peoples of the eastern countries are mostly Muslims.

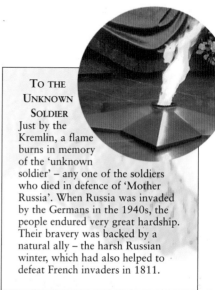

TO THE UNKNOWN SOLDIER Just by the Kremlin, a flame burns in memory of the 'unknown soldier' – any one of the soldiers who died in defence of 'Mother Russia'. When Russia was invaded by the Germans in the 1940s, the people endured very great hardship. Their bravery was backed by a natural ally – the harsh Russian winter, which had also helped to defeat French invaders in 1811.

51

GREENLAND

LINCOLN
SEA

ARCTIC
OCEAN

Ellesmere
Island

G R E E N L A N D

Melville Island

Devon Island

BAFFIN BAY

Banks Island

BEAUFORT
SEA

Prince
of Wales
Island

Victoria Island

Baffin Island

D a v i s   S t r a i t

ALASKA (U.S.A.)

Dawson

Norman Wells

Great Bear
Lake

FOXE BASIN

LABRADOR
SEA

YUKON
TERRITORY

MACKENZIE MOUNTAINS

Mackenzie

N O R T H W E S T   T E R R I T O R I E S

Southampton
Island

Hudson Strait

Mt. Logan
5,951 m

Whitehorse

Dubawnt
Lake

Coats Island

Mansel Island

Ungava
Peninsula

HORN
MOUNTAINS

Yellowknife

ROCKY

Liard

Great Slave Lake
Fort Resolution

Fort Smith

HUDSON BAY

Feuilles

CARIBOU
MOUNTAINS

Lake
Athabasca

BRITISH
COLUMBIA

MOUNTAINS

Peace

C A N A D A

Reindeer
Lake

Churchill

Churchill

Belcher Islands

La Grande Rivière

OTISH
MOUNTAINS

Prince Rupert

COAST MOUNTAINS

Prince George

Peace River

ALBERTA

Nelson

JAMES
BAY

QUEEN
CHARLOTTE
ISLANDS

Edmonton

MANITOBA

Akimiski
Island

Périboncca

Fraser

N. Saskatchewan

Prince Albert

Severn

Vancouver
Island

Kamloops

Red Deer

Lake
Winnipegosis

Lake
Winnipeg

Albany

QUEBEC

St. La

Vancouver

Calgary

Saskatoon

O N T A R I O

Quebec

Fre

Victoria

Medicine Hat

SASKATCHEWAN

Lake
Manitoba

S. Saskatchewan

Regina

Winnipeg

Lake Nipigon

Montreal

U N I T E D   S T A T E S   O F   A M E R I C A

Thunder Bay

Ottawa

Lake Superior

Georgian Bay

Lake Huron

Toronto

Lake Ontario

Hamilton

Niagara Falls

Windsor

Lake Erie

CANADA

GREENLAND AND
CANADA

The North American Arctic is a deep-frozen land of ice and rock, of sea inlets and remote islands. It includes Greenland and northern Canada. Canada extends southwards to the United States border. It is bounded in the west by the Pacific Ocean and the American state of Alaska, and in the east by the Atlantic Ocean.

*▶ Across the ice
The traditional
means of transport
in the Arctic was
the dog sled. Sleds
are still used, although
today most people use
a snowmobile or
Skidoo
instead.*

Separated from the North American mainland by the Davis Strait, Greenland (or Kallaalit Nunaat) is a territory of Denmark, but now has complete home rule. This is the world's biggest island, but inland most of the land is buried under permanent ice. The population lives around the coast and numbers only about 55,000. Most are Inuit (Eskimo), with a minority of Scandinavian or mixed descent. The chief industries are fishery and fish-processing. There are plans to prospect for minerals and to develop tourism.

Another European possession in the North American continent is the little island territory of St Pierre and Miquelon, which is ruled by France.

Canada is the second largest country in the world, and yet it is home to only 30 million people. Most Canadians live in the big,

bustling cities of the far south, such as Montréal, Toronto and, in the far west, Vancouver. The capital and home of the Canadian parliament is the smaller city of Ottawa, in southeastern Ontario.

Canada's southeastern provinces include Newfoundland and Labrador, and the 'Maritimes' (Nova Scotia, New Brunswick and Prince Edward Island). Canada's fishing grounds on the foggy North Atlantic were once the world's richest, but have declined disastrously in recent years.

The huge southern provinces of Québec and Ontario take in the St Lawrence River and its Seaway, an engineered link which makes it possible for

◄ *Lumber for the sawmills*
Great rafts of felled tree trunks are floated down the Coulonge, a tributary of the Ottawa River in southwest Québec province.

▶ *Toronto skyline*
Toronto, on Lake Ontario, is Canada's biggest city, with a population of 3,893,000. Its skyline is dominated by the 553-metre CN Tower.

ocean-going ships to reach the big cities of the Great Lakes. In the north these provinces border Hudson Bay, along a vast rim of ancient rock called the Canadian Shield. The prairies, natural grasslands which extend across the United States border, are given over to wheat and cattle farming. Prairie provinces include Manitoba, Saskatchewan and Winnipeg. Beyond the snowy peaks of the Rocky Mountains, the mild, moist climate of British Columbia supports large areas of evergreen forest.

The severe climate makes it hard for people to live in the northern wilderness, which stretches across Yukon Territory, Northwest Territories (NWT) and Nunavut, the vast Inuit homeland which will break away from NWT in 1999. Here, a broad belt of spruce forest gives way to bare, deep frozen soil called tundra.

Canada's wilderness areas are home to polar bears and seals, caribou, moose, beavers and loons. They also have valuable resources, providing timber, hydroelectric power and minerals, including oil. Most Canadians enjoy a high standard of living. Since 1994 Canada has been a member of the North American Free Trade Agreement (NAFTA).

The original Canadians crossed into North America from Asia long ago, when the two continents were joined by land. They were ancestors of the peoples now known in the United States as Native Americans and in Canada as First Peoples. They were followed by the Inuit people of the Arctic. Today these two groups make up only four percent of Canada's population. Many have kept their languages and traditions alive, but have also suffered from poverty and from the development of their

▶ *As far as the eye can see*
A field of golden wheat stretches to the horizon in the prairie province of Saskatchewan – one of the world's great grain-producing regions, or 'breadbaskets'.

traditional hunting grounds and fisheries.

In the 1500s eastern Canada was explored and settled by French and British fur-traders and fishermen. In the 1700s the French and British battled to control Canada, and it ended up as a dominion, or self-ruling nation, within the British empire. Today, about 40 per cent of Canadians are descended from peoples of the British Isles, especially Scots. People of French descent make up 27 per cent, and there are also many other minorities, including Ukrainians, Germans, Scandinavians, Chinese, Vietnamese and Afro-Caribbeans.

Canada has two official languages, French and English, and over the last 35 years many people in the French-speaking province of Québec have campaigned to become separate from the rest of Canada. Most Canadians are

MAPLE LEAF COUNTRY

The emblem of Canada is the leaf of the maple tree, which appears on the national flag. Various types of maple grow in Canada. Sugar maples are grown in Ontario, Québec and New Brunswick. The sweet, sticky sap is collected and boiled to make natural maple syrup or sirop d'érable – an invention of the Native American peoples of this region. It is delicious served with pancakes or ice cream.

Christians. French-speakers are mostly Roman Catholic and English-speakers are mostly Protestant.

Because most Canadian cities are so near the USA, American influences on the way of life have been very strong. Even so, Canadians like to do things in their own way and take pride in their differences. Canada has made an international name for itself in sports such as ice hockey, in literature, cinema and popular music.

◀ *Ice hockey*
Ice hockey was first played in Canada, and is still hugely popular. Major teams include the Montréal Canadiens and the Toronto Maple Leafs.

▲ *In the blue Canadian Rockies*
A brimming lake, forests of spruce and tamarack (a kind of larch), and snowy peaks make up the classic landscape of Alberta.

ALASKA (U.S.A.)

Pt. Barrow
Barrow
ARCTIC COASTAL PLAIN
Colville
BROOKS RANGE
Noatak
Kobuk
Koyukuk
Fort Yukon
Bering Strait
Tanana
Fairbanks
St. Lawrence Island
Nome
Mt. McKinley
Tanana
Holy Cross
Anchorage
Cordova
CANADA
Nunivak Island
Bethel
Kenai
Seward
Juneau
GULF OF ALASKA
Sitka
Homer
Ketchikan
BRISTOL BAY
Kodiak
Kodiak Island
Alaska Peninsula
ALEUTIAN ISLANDS
Rat Is.
Andreanof Is.
Fox Is.

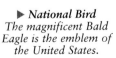

▶ **National Bird**
The magnificent Bald Eagle is the emblem of the United States.

THE UNITED STATES OF AMERICA

▶ **Wrestling a steer**
Rodeos are a chance to show off ranching skills. The cowboys and pioneers of the 1800s are still heroes to many Americans.

UNITED STATES OF AMERICA

The United States of America (USA) make up a huge country which straddles eight time zones. It extends across the North American continent from the Pacific to the Atlantic Oceans, from Canada south to Mexico. It includes great cities which light up the night sky, as well as large areas of remote wilderness and virgin forest.

The northeastern part of the United States has a mild climate, although winter snowfall can be heavy and summers can be very warm. Inland from the rocks and stormy shores of the Atlantic coast are the woodlands of New England, which turn to every shade of red and gold in the autumn. Here there are broad rivers and neat little towns dating back to the days of the early European settlers, and also the historic city of Boston, Massachusetts. In the far north the Great Lakes mark the border with Canada. On this border are the spectacular Niagara Falls, a major tourist attraction which also provides valuable hydroelectric power. The Appalachian mountain ranges run for 2,400 kilometres from north to south, through the eastern United States.

The northeast of the USA include centres of industry and mining, and large cities with gleaming skyscrapers, sprawling suburbs, road and rail networks. New York City, centred on the island of Manhattan, is the business capital of the USA and also a lively centre of arts and entertainment. To many people, New York City is a symbol of America – fast-moving and energetic, a melting pot of different peoples and cultures. The northern city of Detroit is a centre of the motor industry, and Chicago, on the shores of Lake Michigan, is another bustling city of skyscrapers, a centre of business and manufacture.

Travelling south from the Delaware River and the great city of Philadelphia, you come to the Potomac River and the federal District of Columbia (DC), the site of Washington,

◄ **Welcome to Boston!**
Boston, the state capital of Massachussets, has a large population of Italian and Irish Americans. It is the chief commercial and industrial centre of New England.

capital city of the United States. Approaching the American South, you pass into warmer country where tobacco and cotton are grown in the red earth. The long peninsula of Florida extends southwards into the Caribbean Sea, fringed by sandy islands called keys. Along the Gulf coast the climate is hot and very humid, with creeks known as bayous and tangled swamps which are home to alligators. Hurricanes are common in late summer and autumn. New Orleans, the home of jazz, has many picturesque old buildings with wrought-iron verandahs. It lies 170 kilometres above the mouth of the Mississippi River, which together with the mighty Missouri drains the centre of the continent. Texas is a huge state which borders Mexico along the Rio Grande. Dry and dusty, it makes its living from cattle ranching and oil.

Prairies once covered the great plains of the Midwest, the home of vast herds of bison or buffalo.

▲ **Baseball country**
Baseball is an all-American invention. Once the ball has been hit, the player must run from base to base around a diamond-shaped pitch.

▼ **Grand Canyon, Arizona**
A glowing panorama stretches out from the north rim of the Grand Canyon. The canyon was shaped by the waters of the Colorado River.

Today the grasslands are largely given over to farming vegetable crops, maize and wheat, or to cattle ranching. Barren, stony 'badlands' rise towards the rugged Rocky Mountain ranges, which form the backbone of the USA as they stretch from the Canadian border south to Mexico.

Southwards and westwards again there are large areas of burning desert, salt flats and canyons, where over the ages the rocks have been worn into fantastic shapes by wind and water. In places, Arizona's spectacular Grand Canyon is 24 kilometres wide and two kilometres deep.

Badwater, in Calfornia's harsh Death Valley, is the lowest point in the United States, 86 metres below sea level.

The Sierra,

Cascade and Coast ranges run parallel with the beautiful Pacific coast. The warm beaches, pines and gigantic redwood trees of California stretch northwards to the rainy and cool ferny forests of Oregon and Washington State. Irrigation has made it possible to farm large areas of California, which produce citrus fruits and grape vines. Major cities of the west include Los Angeles, which takes in the world-famous film studios of Hollywood, beautiful San Francisco, set on a wide bay which can be warm and sparkling blue or shrouded in cool sea-fog, and the busy northern port of Seattle.

The United States has a northern outpost in oil-rich Alaska, its largest state. Alaska

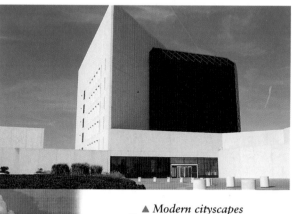

▲ *Modern cityscapes*
Dallas, in the state of Texas, is a business centre for the oil and cotton trade. Skyscrapers were invented in the USA, and many cities are dominated by modern architecture.

was purchased from Russia in 1867. Bordered by Canada, the Alaskan wilderness stretches into the remote Arctic, a deep frozen land of mountains and tundra. Its islands are inhabited by large grizzly bears and its waters by schools of migrating whales. Mount McKinley, at 6,194 metres, is the highest point not just in the United States, but in all of North America. Far to the west, in the Pacific Ocean, the Hawaiian Islands are also part of the USA. Tourists come here to enjoy the warm climate, surf and the islands' spectacular volcanoes.

The United States also governs or has special links with various other territories, such as American Samoa, the Northern Marianas and the Midway Islands in the Pacific Ocean, and Puerto Rico and the US Virgin Islands in the Caribbean.

Native American peoples were the first to settle North America, migrating from Asia possibly as

▲ *Wide open spaces*
A car follows a lonely road through Monument Valley, on the Arizona-Utah border – the homeland of the Navajo people.

early as 30,000 years ago. From the 1500s onwards Native American lands were seized and settled by colonists from Europe. In 1776 the British colonies in the east declared their independence, and during the 1800s their new country, the United States of America, grew rapidly as it gained territory from France, Mexico and Russia. Today, in addition to the small Native American population, there are Americans whose ancestors originally came from Britain, Ireland, Italy, France, Germany, the Netherlands and Poland.

JAMBALAYA!
Rice, seafood, green peppers and hot spices make up this delicious dish from steamy New Orleans, in Louisiana. The inhabitants of this city include many people of French and African descent, and these influences are reflected in its cooking.

60

There are African Americans, whose ancestors were brought to America to work as slaves. There are Jews, Armenians, Spanish, Chinese, Cubans, Hawaiians, Vietnamese and Koreans. All are citizens of the United States.

The nation today is a federation of 50 states, which have the power to pass many of their own laws. The federal seat of government is at the capital, Washington DC. Here is the Congress, made up of a Senate and a House of Representatives, and the White House, the home of the US Presidents.

▶ *Surf's up!*
Surfing is popular in California and in the state of Hawaii, in the Pacific. It is said that the Polynesian inhabitants of Hawaii invented the sport long ago.

The American economy is the most powerful in the world and its influences are felt globally. The country is rich in minerals, including oil, coal and iron ore. American companies produce computers and software, aircraft, cars, and processed foods and there are also many large banks and finance companies. America is the leader in space exploration and technology. Films and television programmes made in Hollywood have made the American way of life very influential around the world. American hamburgers and soft drinks are now bought in many other countries. Popular sports include American football, baseball and basketball.

The USA has close economic links with its neighbours, Canada and Mexico, through the North American Free Trade Agreement (NAFTA) of 1994. It is also a member of many other international groupings, such as the Organization of American States (OAS) and the North Atlantic Treaty Organization (NATO), a military alliance which links it with Western and Central Europe.

KAUAI
Lihue
Kauai Channel
OAHU
AU
MOLOKAI
Honolulu
Wailuku
LANAI
MAUI
Lanai City
KAHOOLAWE
Alenuihaha Channel
Mauna Kea 4,205m
HAWAII
Hilo
Mauna Loa 4,169m

SOUTH AMERICA

BAHAMAS

UNITED STATES OF AMERICA

JAMAICA

HAITI

ANTIGUA AND BARBUDA

BELIZE

HONDURAS

PUERTO RICO

DOMINICA

PANAMA

CUBA

BAHAMAS

Tijuana Mexicali
Ensenada
Ciudad Juárez

Cedros I.

Hermosillo   Chihuahua

Torreón
La Paz   Culiacán   Saltillo   Monterrey   Matamoros
Durango
San Luis Potosí
Aguascalientes   Tampico
Cape Corrientes   Guadalajara   León
Manzanillo   L. de Chapala
MEXICO   Mexico City   Bay of   Campeche
Puebla   Campeche   Yucatán
Acapulco   Orizaba   Veracruz   Peninsula
5,700 m   Terminos
Balsas   Coatzacoalcos   Lagoon
Oaxaca   Villahermosa
Gulf of   **GUATEMALA**
Tehuantepec   Guatemala City
San Salvador
EL SALVADOR
Managua

Rio Grande
Rio Bravo del Norte

SIERRA MADRE

SIERRA MADRE

Gulf of California

Baja California

GULF OF MEXICO

Yucatán Channel

Havana   **CUBA**   Camagüey
Isla de la   Santiago
Juventad   de Cuba
Cayman   Port-au-Prince
Islands (U.K.)   **JAMAICA**   Kingston

Belize City
BELIZE   Belmopan
HONDURAS
Tegucigalpa
NICARAGUA
Lake
Nicaragua
Mosquitos
Gulf
San José
COSTA RICA   Panama City
Gulf of
Panama

B A H A M A S
Nassau
Andros I.
Turks & Caicos Islands (U.K.)

DOMIN REPU
HAITI
CARIBB SEA

PANAMA

COLOMBIA

PACIFIC OCEAN

MEXICO

DOMINICAN REPUBLIC

GRENADA

ST VINCENT AND GRENADINES

BARBADOS

ST KITTS AND NEVIS

EL SALVADOR

TRINIDAD AND TOBAGO

COSTA RICA

NICARAGUA

GUATEMALA

ST LUCIA

62

MEXICO,
CENTRAL AMERICA & THE CARIBBEAN

Mexico stretches southwards from the United States border, meeting the Pacific Ocean in the west and the Gulf of Mexico in the east. To the south are seven small nations – Guatemala, Belize, Honduras, El Salvador, Nicaragua, Costa Rica and Panama. To the east, tropical islands form a large arc around the Caribbean Sea.

Mexico forms a large triangle of land, with a tropical climate. A long thin peninsula, Baja California, runs parallel to the northeast coast. Another broader peninsula, Yucatán, sticks up like a thumb below the Gulf of Mexico. Mexico is a mountainous country, crossed by three branches of the Sierra Madre range. It is a land of deserts, tropical forests and volcanoes, dotted with the spectacular ruins of ancient Native American civilizations, such as the Maya, Toltec and Aztec. Mexico City,

built on the site of an ancient Aztec city, is a vast, polluted, sprawling centre of population. Earthquakes are common.

Today's Mexicans are descended from Native American peoples as well as from the Spanish who invaded and settled the region in the 1500s. Modern Mexico is an oil-producing country and attracts many tourists. It is a member of the North American Free Trade Agreement (NAFTA). However, many Mexicans remain very poor. Over the years many have headed north across the Rio Grande to seek illegal work in the USA.

To the south of Mexico, the mainland tapers to a thin strip of land called the Isthmus of Panama, which since 1914 has been crossed by the

Virgin Is.
(U.K & U.S.)
ANTIGUA &
BARBUDA
n Juan
ST. KITTS
& NEVIS
Montserrat (U.K.)
erto
(U.S.)
Guadeloupe (FR.)
DOMINICA

Martinique (FR.)
ST. LUCIA
BARBADOS
ST. VINCENT &
THE GRENADINES
GRENADA

herlands
ntilles
TRINIDAD
& TOBAGO

◄ *Colour and craft*
This decorative craft work comes from the Jamaican tourist resort of Negril. It is probably inspired by the brilliantly coloured fish of the Caribbean coral reefs.

Atlantic–Pacific shipping link of the Panama Canal. The seven small countries of Central America were also once ruled by Spain and they too have populations descended from Native American peoples as well as Spanish. They live mostly by farming tropical crops such as bananas, coffee and sugar cane. The many poor people of the region have long been exploited by small numbers of the very rich and by brutal dictators. Central America has a long history of political strife and civil war.

The most widespread of the many languages spoken in Central America is Spanish. Most of the population is Roman Catholic. The whole region shares a love of music and dance, of poetry and political argument. Foods of the region have changed little since the days of the Aztecs, and include pancake-like tortillas, crisp tacos, beans, chili peppers and avocados.

To the east, the Caribbean Sea is an arm of the Atlantic Ocean which is dotted with beautiful islands in warm, blue seas. They form two main island chains. The Greater Antilles include Cuba, Jamaica, Hispaniola (occupied by Haiti and the Dominican Republic) and Puerto Rico. The Lesser Antilles are more numerous, but smaller. They include the Virgin Islands, the Leeward and Windward Islands, Barbados and (along the South American coast) Trinidad and Tobago, Aruba and the Netherlands Antilles.

Cuba is the largest Caribbean island, famous for its sugar cane, rum and cigars. Since 1959 Cuba has had a communist government led by Fidel Castro. This has irritated Cuba's powerful neighbour to the north, the

◀ *Fancy ropework*
Based on traditional techniques, this Mexican showman demonstrates lassoing skills for an audience.

◀ *A tropical paradise*
The island of St John is an unspoiled national park within the US Virgin Islands. It has a population of about 3,500.

United States, which forbids trade with the island. Florida, in the USA, has become a haven for Cuban exiles.

The Caribbean region as a whole was once home to Native American peoples such as the Arawaks and the Caribs, after whom the region is named. Then came European invaders, explorers and pirates, including the Spanish, Dutch, French and British. Most of today's Caribbean peoples are descended from West Africans who were brought in as slaves by the Europeans. Many small Caribbean islands became independent after the 1960s, but some remain dependencies of other countries.

Caribbean islanders live by fishing, farming, manufacture and tourism. Favourite sports include baseball in Cuba and cricket in Jamaica and Barbados. The region is famous for its spectacular carnivals, which have encouraged a range of popular music styles, from calypso to salsa, from reggae to soca.

FACES OF ANCIENT MEXICO

This stone figure of a warrior is from the ancient Toltec capital of Tula, on the edge of Mexico's dry, northern regions. It is about 1,000 years old. The ancient civilizations of 'Mesoamerica' (Middle America) were among the greatest achievements of the Native American peoples who migrated southwards through the continent tens of thousands of years ago.

▲ *Going to market, Guatemala*
The Maya people still live in Guatemala. Their women weave beautiful textiles, the patterns varying from one village to another.

65

Point. Gallinas

Barranquilla
Cartagena

▲ Cristobal Colón
5,775 m

COLOMBIA

PANAMA

Cauca

Magdalena

A N D E S

VENEZUELA

Meta

ECUADOR

Cape
Corrientes

Medellin

Pereira   Manizales
Ibagué

Buenaventura

Bogotá

COLOMBIA

Guaviare

Cali   Neiva
Nevado del Huila
5,750 m

Pasto

Point
Galera

Quito

ECUADOR

Chimborazo
6,267 m

Guayaquil

Gulf of
Guayaquil

Point
Aguja

Piura

Chiclayo

Caquetá

Putumayo

Amazon

Iquitos

Marañón

BRAZIL

M O U N T A I N S

Ucayali

Trujillo

Chimbote

▲ Nevado Huascarán
6,768 m

PERU

Callao

Lima

Huancayo

Paracas
Pen.

Nazca

Cuzco

Volcán
El Misti
5,842 m

Arequipa ▲

Nevado
Ancohume
▲ 6,550 m

Lake
Titicaca

La Paz

BOLIVIA

Mamoré

Guaporé

Cochabamba

Santa Cruz

PACIFIC
OCEAN

Oruro

Lake
Poopó

Sucre

PERU

A L T I P L A N O

Potosí

Pilcomayo

CHILE

PARAGUAY

BOLIVIA

▽ **Mask of gold**
*Rumours of gold treasure
brought Spanish invaders t
the Andes in 1532. They
defeated and plundered th
great Inca empire.*

THE NORTHERN ANDES

The Andes mountains extend down the whole length of South America, from north to south. They rise in Colombia, the country which borders the narrow land link with Central America, the Isthmus of Panama. The northern Andes continue to run parallel with the Pacific coast, through Ecuador, Peru and Bolivia.

▲ *A woman of the Bora*
The Bora are one of the indigenous peoples who live between the Caueta and Putumayo rivers in Colombia.

Colombia is a beautiful country, with coasts on both the Caribbean Sea and the Pacific Ocean. It takes in southwestern rainforests as well as dry, dusty lands and grassy plains. The mountains dominate the country, forming three main ranges. They are mined for gold, emeralds, salt and coal. Coffee is grown in the foothills.

The chief cities of Colombia are either on the Caribbean coast, which is warm and humid, or in the cooler mountain regions. The latter include Medellín and the capital, Bogotá, which lies in the Cundinamarca basin, surrounded by peaks of the eastern range. The coca plant, used to make a dangerous drug called cocaine, is grown in parts of the countryside. The illegal trade in cocaine has created a problem of crime and gang warfare in the cities.

The Andes rise to 6,267 metres above sea level at Chimborazo in Ecuador. This country's name means 'Equator' in Spanish, and the Pacific coast around the Equator is hot and moist. Bananas and sugar cane are grown here. In the cooler foothills of the Andes coffee is an important crop. The capital is Quito, sited on a plateau at 2,850 metres above sea level. To the east of the mountains are rainforests,

▲ *The biggest lake in South America*
Lake Titicaca is 3,810 metres above sea
level. Rushes which grow in the lake
are used to make houses and boats.

where oil is drilled.

Ecuador also governs the remote Galapagos Islands, which lie about 1,000 kilometres to the west, in the Pacific Ocean. The islands have a remarkable wildlife, which includes giant tortoises and marine iguanas (sea lizards).

In the 1400s, Peru was the centre of the mighty Inca empire. This advanced Native American civilization produced beautiful textiles and jewellery in gold and precious stones. It was destroyed when the region was invaded by the Spanish in 1532. Ruined Inca cities such as Machu Picchu still perch high amongst the peaks of the Andes. Terraced hillsides allow crops such as potatoes to be grown in the mountains. The Peruvian Andes soar to 6,768 metres above sea level at Huascarán. Fishing is important along the foggy Pacific coast. In the far east, rivers flow through tropical forests into the Amazon.

Lake Titicaca lies high in the Andes, on the border with Bolivia. This inland country lies across the high plateau of the Altiplano and the

◀ *The sure-footed*
llama
The llama is used
for carrying goods
in the Andes. This
beast can pick its
way along the
narrowest of
mountain
paths.

humid eastern forests. The city of La Paz is the world's highest capital city, at 3,660 metres above sea level. Bolivia actually has twin capitals. La Paz is the seat of government, while Sucre, to the south, is the legal centre of the nation. Bolivia produces tin, timber, rubber and potatoes.

The lands of the northern Andes are home to many Native American peoples, such as the Quechua and Aymara, and their languages, crafts, customs and music have all survived. The

▽ *Sounds of the Andes*
Native American traditions are kept alive in music. Popular instruments include the pan-pipes or rondador, drums, guitars and flutes.

◄ *In Peru's misty mountains*
The Urumbaba river flows through steep gorges below the twin peaks of Machu Picchu and Huayna Picchu.

▼ *Baby pouch, Cuzco style*
This mother and baby belong to the Quechua, a people who live around the old Inca capital of Cuzco, in Peru.

whole region was ruled by Spain from the 1500s to the early 1800s, when revolutionaries such as the Venezuelan Simón Bolívar secured independence. Many people are of Spanish or mixed descent. Spanish is spoken throughout the region as well as a number of Native American languages. Most Northern Andeans are Roman Catholics, although the colourful festivals and pilgrimages of the region often show a clear link with Native American beliefs.

Although the region is rich in minerals and timber, many ordinary farmers and miners live in great poverty. This has led to political unrest and guerrilla warfare in many regions during the last 30 years.

WILDLIFE OF THE ANDES
The most famous bird of the mountains is the Andean condor, the world's largest flying bird. It uses rising air currents to soar to heights of 4,000 metres on its huge wings. The shaggy-furred spectacled bear, which lives on the densely forested lower slopes of the Andes, takes its name from the markings around its eyes.

SOUTH AMERICA

VENEZUELA

GUYANA

SURINAM

▶ *Scarves and frills*
This Brazilian woman from the coastal city of Salvador de Bahía, on Brazil's Atlantic coast, wears the traditional costume of the region for a festival.

FRENCH GUIANA

Gulf of Venezuela

Netherlands Antilles

Maracaibo

Caracas

Port of Spain **TRINIDAD & TOBAGO**

Lake Maracaibo

ANDES MTS.

Barcelona

Pico Bolívar 5,002 m

LLANOS

Orinoco

Orinoco Delta

VENEZUELA

Angel Falls

Georgetown

Paramaribo

COLOMBIA

G U I A N A

H I G H L A N D S

GUYANA

Orinoco

SURINAM

Cayenne

FRENCH GUIANA

Branco

Pico da Neblina 3014 m

Negro

Japurá

Macapá

Marajó Bay

Marajó I.

São Marcos Bay

A m a z o n

Manaus

Santarém

Belém

São Luis

S E L V A S

Madeira

Tapajós

Xingu

Tocantins

Teresina

Fortaleza

Juruá

Purus

Aripuanã

Parnaiba

SE

Jiparaná

PERU

Rio Branco

SERRA DOS PARECIS
Guapore

Arinos

BRAZIL

Araguaia

Sobradinho Reservoir

São Fra

BOLIVIA

MATO GROSSO PLATEAU

Cuiabá

Brasília

Goiânia

Salvador

Campo Grande

BRAZILIAN HIGHLANDS

Uberlândia

Paraná

Belo Horizonte

PARAGUAY

São Paulo

Campos

Rio de Janeiro

Cape Frio

Itaipu Res.

Santos

S E R R A

D O

M A R

Itaguaçu Falls

Curitiba

ARGENTINA

Uruguay

Florianópolis

Santa Maria

Pôrto Alegre

Patos Lagoon

URUGUAY

Mirim Lake

BRAZIL

70

BRAZIL
AND ITS NEIGHBOURS

Brazil is South America's largest nation. It takes in the world's largest surviving area of rainforest, around the River Amazon. To the north, Venezuela lies on the River Orinoco, which flows into the Caribbean Sea. Three smaller countries also border the Caribbean coast – Guyana, Surinam and French Guiana.

About a third of Brazil is taken up by tropical rainforests. These are crossed by hundreds of rivers, which drain into the wide, muddy waters of the Amazon, one of the world's two longest rivers. The river basin of the Amazon is the world's largest, covering 7,045,000 square kilometres. All kinds of rare plants, parrots, snakes and monkeys live in the dense, dripping rainforests, which are under threat from road builders, farmers, miners and loggers.

Brazil is a vast country which also includes tropical grasslands, fertile plateaus and dry areas of scrub. Brazilian farmlands are the world's biggest suppliers of coffee and of soya beans, and the country is a major exporter of orange juice and sugar.

Most Brazilians live in the big cities of the Atlantic coast, such as Rio de Janeiro and São Paulo. The country has rich resources, but many of the population are poor people who live in shacks built on the city outskirts. Brasília, with its broad avenues and high-rise buildings, was specially built as a new capital in the 1960s. Portuguese is the chief language of Brazil. The land formed part of Portugal's overseas empire from 1500 until 1822. The original inhabitants included

▲ *Carnival in Rio*
For five days each year the Brazilian city of Rio de Janeiro is taken over by carnival dancers wearing spectacular costumes.

◀ **To the glory of God**
Nine out of ten Brazilians are Roman Catholics. This remarkable building is the Metropolitan Cathedral in Brasília, the modern capital.

a great variety of Native American peoples and cultures. Many of these were destroyed by European diseases, by persecution and murder. Scores of Brazil's surviving indigenous peoples, such as the Yanomami, face great problems today. Large numbers of Brazilians are of mixed descent, many of European origin (including Portuguese, Italian and German), others of African origin.

The city of Rio de Janeiro has one of the world's most famous carnivals, which people celebrate to the rhythms of a dance called the samba. The national passion is association football, and Brazil has one of the most successful national teams in the world.

To the northeast of Brazil, on the Caribbean coast, is Venezuela. This land, crossed by the Orinoco River, includes rainforests, high mountains and

the tropical grassy plains of the Llanos. The beautiful Angel Falls (the highest in the world, with a drop of 979 metres) provide hydroelectric power, while Lake

▼ **Coffee for the world**
Coffee beans of the finest quality are grown in the Brazilian states of São Paolo, Paraná Espírito Santo and Minas Gerais.

Maracaibo, in the northwest, is rich in oil. Its capital is the northern city of Carácas. Venezuela was formerly ruled by Spain, and Spanish remains its chief language.

The three other countries on the Caribbean coast are Guyana, Surinam and French Guiana. The first was once a British colony, the second was a Dutch colony and the third is still an overseas department of France. Most people live in the humid regions of the coast, while the rainforests

▶ *What a mouth!* Razor-toothed piranha fish live in South America's muddy rivers. They are very fierce and can strip the flesh from a bone in seconds.

and mountains of the remote south are more sparsely populated. Crops include sugar cane, coffee, rice and bananas. The Demerara river of Guyana has given its name to a famous type of brown sugar, while a type of hot red pepper is named after Cayenne, the capital of French Guiana. An important mineral resource of the region is bauxite, used in the making of aluminium. Kourou in French Guiana is a launch site for the Ariane rockets of the European Space Agency.

Many different ethnic groups live in these northern regions of the continent. They include Native American peoples, who like the Amazonian groups to the south, have had to struggle to survive. There are also Afro-Caribbeans, Asians and Europeans, all of whom have mingled over the years.

BENEATH THE SUGAR LOAF
Sugar Loaf Mountain towers above the port of Rio de Janeiro, topped by a statue of Jesus Christ with outstretched arms. Rio occupies a beautiful position on Guanabara Bay, but this sprawling city of nearly 10 million people includes large areas of slums and shanty towns. Rio was formerly the capital of Brazil.

► *The armour-plated mammals* There are 20 species of armadillo scattered through South America. Their skin is covered in horny plates. They hunt insects, snakes and lizards.

Arica
Iquique
ATACAMA DESERT
Calama
BOLIVIA
Antofagasta
CHACO
Verde
Pilcomayo
Concepción
PARAGUAY
Salta
Asunción
Cuidad del Este
GRAN
Bermejo
Ojos del Salado 6,880 m
San Miguel de Tucumán
Formosa
Copiapó
Santiago del Estero
Resistencia
Alto Paraná
Catamarca
Corrientes
Posadas
La Rioja
Salado
MESOPOTAMIA
Paraná
Coquimbo
Mar Chiquito
Paraguay
Pta. Lengua de Vaca
San Juan
Córdoba
Concordia
Salto
Uruguay
Aconcagua 6,959 m
Santa Fe
Paysandú
Valparaiso
Mendoza
Rosario
Paraná
Negro
Rancagua
Santiago
San Luis
Río Cuarto
Buenos Aires
URUGUAY
San Rafael
La Plata
Montevideo
Talca
Salado
PAMPAS
Río de La Plata
Pta. Norte
Cape San Antonio
Chillán
ARGENTINA
Mar del Plata
Concepción
Pta. Lavapié
Bahia Blanca
Cape Corrientes
CHILE
Neuquén
Colorado
Bahía Blanca
Temuco
Negro
Valdivia
Limay
Viedma
Pta. de la Galera
San Matias Gulf
Osorno
PATAGONIA
Puerto Montt
Valdés Peninsula
Chiloé I.
Chubut
Rawson
C. Quilán
Chico
ANDES MOUNTAINS
SIERRA DE CORDOBA
LOS CHONOS ARCHIPELAGO
Comodoro Rivadavia
Lake Buenos Aires
San Jorge Gulf
Deseado
C. Tres Puntas
Puerto Deseado
Penas Gulf
PACIFIC OCEAN
Chico
Wellington I.
Santa Cruz
Puerto Santa Cruz
FALKLAND/MALVINAS ISLANDS
Bahía Grande
West Falkland
Stanley
Río Gallegos
East Falkland
REINA ADELAIDA ARCHIPELAGO
Strait of Magellan
Punta Arenas
Tierra del Fuego
Santa Inés I.
Ushuaia
C. San Diego
Cape Horn
BRAZIL

PARAGUAY

URUGUAY

ARGENTINA

CHILE

FALKLAND ISLANDS

SOUTH GEORGIA (U.K

ARGENTINA
AND ITS NEIGHBOURS

The southern Andes mountains run down the border between Chile and Argentina to the cold and stormy waters of Tierra del Fuego and Cape Horn. This region includes some of the driest deserts in the world, bleak plateaus, sunny valleys and rolling grasslands. Uruguay and Paraguay lie between Argentina and Brazil.

Argentina is the largest country in the southern part of South America. Its capital is Buenos Aires on the River Plate. More than eight out of every ten Argentineans are city dwellers. However it was the country's cattle-farming regions – the Pampa grasslands and the northeast – that in the last 150 years brought wealth to the country and attracted large numbers of settlers from Europe.

The Pampas were famed in the 1800s as the home of Argentina's wild cowboys, the Gauchos. Argentina's northern borders cross the tropical wilderness of the Gran Chaco, while its western borders follow the high peaks of the Andes range, which reach their highest point at Cerro Aconcagua (at 6,959 metres above sea level, the highest peak in all the Americas). In the shelter of the Andes, around the city of Mendoza, the climate is warm enough to grow fruit and grape vines. To the south are the windswept plateaus of Patagonia, largely given over to sheep farming. The port of Ushuaia is the southernmost town in the world.

Far out in the southern Atlantic Ocean are the windswept Falkland Islands, also grazed by large flocks of sheep. They are governed as a British colony but are claimed by Argentina, to whom they are the Islas Malvinas, and were at the centre of a bitter war between Britain and Argentina in 1982.

Northwards from Buenos Aires, across the River Plate, lies Montevideo, capital of Uruguay. This is another country which raises cattle and sheep, and whose rich grasslands and mild climate attracted European settlers. Neighbouring Paraguay is far from any coast. Most of its people have chosen to farm the hills and plains of the east rather than settle in the inhospitable,

◀ **Bottom of the world**
Ushuaia, in Argentina, is the world's most southerly town, just over a thousand kilometres from the North Pole. It has long hours of sunlight during the southern summer, which corresponds to winter in the northern half of the world.

hot region of the Gran Chaco.
To the west of the Andes is Chile, whose shape makes up the longest and narrowest country in this atlas. It includes one of the driest regions on Earth, the Atacama desert. However, it also includes fertile orchards and vineyards, the big capital city of Santiago and the specacular glaciers of the southern Andes. Chile also governs Easter Island, some 1,760 kilometres to the west in the south Pacific Ocean.

Southern South America includes many ancient Native American sites as well as colonial cities founded by Spanish invaders in the 1500s. During the days of rule by Spain many indigenous peoples were destroyed by savage wars or by diseases brought into the country by the Europeans. From the 1800s onwards many

immigrants came to settle in the region as well as the Spanish. They included Italians, Basques, Germans, Central Europeans, Welsh, English and Jewish people. Spanish is spoken throughout the region, alongside other European languages and some surviving Native American languages, such as those of the Guaraní and Mapuche.

Since the countries of the region broke away from Spanish rule in the nineteenth century, they have

▶ **Chilean panorama**
In Chile, the Andes mountain range forms fantastic icy peaks, some of which are active volcanoes.

known great political strife. Rule by military dictators has taken place in Argentina, Chile, Uruguay and Paraguay. In 1973 3,000 Chileans simply 'disappeared' – tortured and murdered by the military when General Pinochet overthrew the elected government. A further 80,000 opponents of Pinochet were imprisoned. Three years later 10,000 Argentineans 'disappeared' at the hands of death squads who supported military rule. Democracy returned to the region in the 1980s, but there are still serious economic problems and cities such as Santiago are ringed by slums and shanty towns.

Argentina and Chile are both countries which love literature, especially poetry. Folk songs and dance are a way of life, influenced both by Spanish and Native American traditions. A dance called the tango, first performed in the slums of Buenos Aires a hundred years ago, went on to become popular around the world. Popular sports include association and rugby football and motor-racing. The horse-riding skills of the Gauchos are re-ennacted in polo, strictly for the wealthy, and in a wild Argentinean sport called pato, which these days is a kind of basketball played on horseback.

The region inherited the Roman Catholic faith from its Spanish rulers, but there are also a growing number of Protestants, as well as Jews and people of other religions.

PLANT LIFE OF THE SOUTH

Southern South America includes a great variety of habitats, from coastal desert to savannah, from cloud forest to evergreen scrub. Plants of the region include all kinds of native species which have been exported to gardens and greenhouses around the world. These include cactuses, nasturtiums, monkey puzzle trees, fuchsias and pampas grass.

ASIA

TURKEY

SYRIA

IRAQ

IRAN

JORDAN

LEBANON

CYPRUS

SAUDI ARABIA

YEMEN

QATAR

BAHRAIN

UNITED ARAB
EMIRATES

KUWAIT

OMAN

78

SOUTH WEST ASIA

This part of Asia includes the lands sometimes called the Near East or the Middle East. It stretches from the shores of the Black Sea southwards to the Arabian peninsula.

Turkey is a large country whose most westerly part, around the beautiful old city of Istanbul, lies in Europe, across a strait called the Bosporus. Turkey has warm shores on the Mediterranean and Black Seas, but inland are grassy plains and mountain ranges which can be bitterly cold in winter. Its eastern neighbour, Iran, was formerly known as Persia. It includes fertile farmland and grasslands along the Caspian Sea, as well as bleak deserts and snowy mountain ranges. Turkey's southern neighbours are Syria and Iraq. They are part of a hot, very dry region. It is only made green by

▶ **Followers of Islam**
This Muslim girl from San'a, the capital of Yemen, wears a black veil over her face.

the courses of two great rivers, the Tigris and Euphrates, which flow southwards into the Persian Gulf.

Southwest Asia's mild Mediterranean region includes the little island of Cyprus and the small nations of Lebanon and Israel, although these do border harsh desert terrain. The shores of the Dead Sea, a salt lake on the Israel-Jordan border, are 400 metres below sea level.

The great block of land known as the Arabian peninsula juts out into the Indian Ocean, with coasts on the Red Sea and the Persian Gulf. This is a region of trackless, shimmering deserts and rocky highlands, which have to be crossed by camel or four-wheel drive vehicles. It is dominated by the

▼ **On the Gulf**
Dubai, an oil port on the Persian Gulf, is an ancient centre of trade and fishing. Its nearby airport is an important stop-off point on international routes.

▲ **Flare up in Iraq**
Natural gas is burned off at well - heads. Iraq's rich oil and gas reserves were one reason behind the Gulf War of 1991.

▶ **Tents in the desert**
Many desert peoples are nomads, following their herds from one seasonal pasture to another. This tent is in Rub' al Khali, Saudi Arabia's 'Empty Quarter'.

▼ **To the glory of God**
This breathtakingly beautiful mosque is in Isfahan, in Iran. It was begun in the year 1612, during the reign of Shah Abbas the Great.

Kingdom of Saudi Arabia, which is fringed by smaller Arab states, including Jordan, Yemen, Oman, the United Arab Emirates (UAE), Qatar, Bahrain and Kuwait.

Southwest Asia produces citrus fruits, dates, olives, nuts, cotton and tobacco. It depends heavily on irrigation in its drier parts. The region's greatest resource by far is oil and natural gas, which has brought great wealth. However these riches have not reached many of the region's poorer people, who live by herding camels and goats or fishing. Traditional crafts include the making of the world's finest carpets in Iran and Turkey.

Southwest Asia has an ancient and fascinating history. The world's first farmers raised animals and grew their crops around the Tigris and Euphrates about 10,000 years ago. Many great towns and cities grew up in the region, and it was also the birthplace of three world religions – Judaism, Christianity and Islam. The city of Jerusalem is holy to all three faiths, while Mecca in Saudi Arabia is the holiest site of Islam and a centre of pilgrimage.

Southwest Asian peoples include Greeks, Turks, Jews and Iranians. The homeland of the Kurdish people is divided between Turkey, Iraq and Iran. Arabs live in much of the region, forming a number of different cultural groups and nationalities, from the Palestinians in the state of Israel to the Marsh Arabs who live in the wetlands of southern Iraq.

The Middle East has always been at a crossroads of cultures, with trading routes stretching

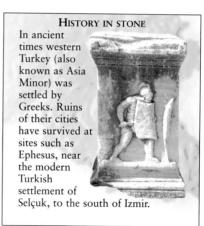

HISTORY IN STONE

In ancient times western Turkey (also known as Asia Minor) was settled by Greeks. Ruins of their cities have survived at sites such as Ephesus, near the modern Turkish settlement of Selçuk, to the south of Izmir.

eastwards to Central Asia and China, westwards to Europe and North Africa, southwards to India and East Africa. Tragically it has also been devastated by wars for much of its history. Recent years have seen war and strife through most of the region, from Cyprus to Israel and Lebanon, to Iraq, Kuwait and Iran.

◀ *A holy city*
Qom, in Iran, is sacred to Moslems of the Shia sect. Religion has played an important part in the government of Iran since the king, or Shah, was overthrown in 1979.

81

AFGHANISTAN

NEPAL

BHUTAN

TURKMENISTAN

TAJIKISTAN

Mazar-e-Sharif

Herat

HINDU

AFGHANISTAN   Kabul

Farah

Khyber Pass   Peshawar

DISPUTED

AREA   K2
8,611m

KARAKORAM

Srinagar

Qandahar   Islamabad

Rawalpindi

JAMMU &
KASHMIR

RIGESTAN
DESERT

Quetta   Faisalabad Lahore

Amritsar

PAKISTAN   Multan   Sutlej   PUNJAB

BALUCHISTAN
PLATEAU   Sukkur Bahawalpur

Tibet (CHINA)

Nanda Devi ▲
7,817m

Delhi

NEPAL

BHUTAN

Karachi   Hyderabad   GREAT INDIAN DESERT
(THAR DESERT)

New Delhi   Bareilly

Annapurna
8,078m ▲

Mt Everest
8,848m ▲

Thimphu

Gulf of Kachch   Indus

Jodhpur   Jaipur   Agra

Lucknow   Ghagara   Katmandu   BHUTAN

Brahmaputra

NAGA HILL

Ajmer   Yamuna   Kanpur

Udaipur   Kota   Gwalior   Allahabad Varanasi   Patna   Gauhati

Jamnagar   Ahmadabad Indore   Bhopal   Son   Jabalpur

Narmada

Asanol

BANGLADESH   Imphal

Khulna   Dhaka

Bhavnagar   Vadodara

Surat

I N D I A   Jamshedpur   Calcutta   Chittagong

Gulf of Khambhat

Aurangabad   Nagpur   Raipur   Cuttack   Mouths of the Ganges

MYANMAR
(BURMA)

Mumbai
(Bombay)   D E C C A N   Mahanadi

Pune   Godavari

Kolhapur   Solapur   Hyderabad

Krishna   Vishakhapatnam

Hubli-Dharwar   Vijayawada

Kurnool

Penner   Nellore

WESTERN   EASTERN GHATS

Mangalore   Bangalore

Mysore   Chennai
(Madras)

Kozhikode   GHATS

Coimbatore

Tiruchchirappalli

Cochin   Madurai   Palk Strait

Jaffna

Trivandrum   Gulf of Mannar   Trincomalee

C. Comorin

SRI LANKA

Colombo   Kandy

Pidurutalagala
2,524m

Galle

MALDIVES

INDIAN
OCEAN

PAKISTAN

BANGLADESH

INDIA

SRI LANKA

MALDIVES

Andam
&
Nicobar
(India

INDIA AND ITS NEIGHBOURS

Southern Asia forms a massive triangle of land which is bordered by the Indian Ocean. It is called the Indian subcontinent. Where it meets the countries to the north, the land has been squeezed up and crumpled, to form the world's highest mountain ranges.

The Karakoram and Himalaya ranges run in a great arc from northern Afghanistan, through northern Pakistan and India to the small mountain kingdoms of Nepal and Bhutan. The peaks soar to 8,848 metres above sea level at Mount Everest or Qomolangma, on the border between Nepal and Tibet (a region governed by China). This is the highest mountain in the world.

Many streams and rivers rise in these snow-capped mountains. The mighty Indus River flows into the Arabian Sea, fed by the Jhelum, Chenab, Ravi and Sutlej waterways which cross Pakistan's Punjab region. The River Ganges flows southeast, crossing the fertile plains of northern India before joining the Brahmaputra in Bangladesh. The Irawaddy, another long river, crosses the country of Myanmar

▼ *Street performers*
A deadly cobra sways to the music of a snake charmer. India's big cities bustle with busy crowds, street vendors, beggars and showmen.

(or Burma) to the east. India is a very large country which includes the forested hills of the Eastern and Western Ghats, sandy deserts, the plateau country of the Deccan and teeming, colourful cities such as Delhi, Bombay and Calcutta. The climate is extremely hot for much of the year, relieved when the monsoon winds bring heavy downpours of rain. Indian Ocean islands include beautiful, tropical Sri Lanka and a long chain of coral reefs and islands, the Maldives. The

▶ *The Taj Mahal, near Agra*
The domes of this great marble tomb are reflected in pools of water. It was completed in 1653.

latter are so low-lying that they could disappear beneath the waves if the world's climate were to become warmer, causing a rise in sea levels.

Crops grown by the farmers of the subcontinent include jute, tea, coconuts, sugarcane, cotton, millet, sorghum and maize. Drought is common in many regions, while coastal regions of Bangladesh often experience severe flooding. Most of the region is rural, but the great cities of India and Pakistan include factories and workshops producing textiles of cotton and silk, heavy machinery, iron and steel. India manufactures computer equipment. Bombay produces films and videos.

The population of India numbers 969,700,000. Pakistan numbers about 137,800,000 and Bangladesh 122,200,000. It is hard to feed so many mouths and poverty is widespread. The mountainous nations to the north and the Maldive islands are thinly populated.

This part of Asia is home to very many different peoples and ancient cultures. About 845 different languages may be heard in India alone. Many religions have also grown up in this region over the

AT THE MARKET
Brilliantly coloured dyes and powders are laid out at a market in the southern Indian city of Mysore. India's street markets offer bright bales of cotton and silk, silver jewellery, carved wooden boxes and trays, statues of Hindu gods, wreaths of flowers and sweet sticks of incense. There are also all kinds of practical goods for sale, such as radios, batteries, pots and pans. Tailors make up shirts, trousers or fine saris. Stalls sell sweet, milky tea as well as delicious snacks.

▶ *The biggest of the cats*
The powerful but increasingly rare Bengal tiger lives in the forests of Nepal, India and Bangladesh. It is protected in special reserves.

▶ *The Buddhist temples of Myanmar*
In ancient times Pagan, the City of a
Thousand Temples, was the capital of
Burma, or Myanmar. Most Burmese still
worship at Buddhist temples today.

ages, including Hinduism,
Buddhism, Sikhism and Jainism.
Afghanistan, the Maldives,
Pakistan and Bangladesh are all
Muslim nations, and many
Muslims also live in India. All
these faiths have inspired a
wealth of religious ceremonies,
dances and festivals.

The Indian subcontinent has
seen many splendid civilisations
come and go, from that of
Mohenjo-Daro (dating back
about 4,500 years) to that of the
Moguls who ruled India from
1526 until the 1800s. India,
Pakistan, Bangladesh,
Myanmar and Sri Lanka all
went on to become part of
the British empire,
but have been
independent
nations since
1947-48.

India today is
the world's largest
democracy. Pakistan and
Myanmar have known
long periods of military

▲ *The holy Ganges*
Hindu pilgrims come to the holy city of
Varanasi, in northern India. They bathe in
the sacred waters of the River Ganges.

rule while Afghanistan has
suffered civil war and many
violent changes of government.
Many peoples from the Indian
subcontinent have, over the ages,
settled in other parts of the
world. There are Indian,
Pakistani or Bangladeshi
communities in Southeast
Asia, East and South Africa,
Great Britain, Canada,
Australia, the Caribbean
and the Pacific.

▶ **On the South China Sea** Traditional wooden sailing ships may still be seen. They are called junks.

NORTH KOREA

SOUTH KOREA

MONGOLIA

RUSSIA

Hovsgol Lake

Ulaangom

Darhan
Edernet
Ulan Bator
Choybalsan
Tamsagbulag

HENTYN MTS.

Qiqihar

Harbin

Mudanjiang

GREATER HINGGAN
LESSER HINGGAN

Amur

Changchun
Jilin
Ch'ongjin
Tonghua
NORTH KOREA

Fushun
Hamhung
Shenyang
P'yongyang
Wonsan

Kaesong
SOUTH KOREA
Seoul
Kwangju
Pusan

KAZAKHSTAN

Fuhai
Hovd

MONGOLIA

HANGAYN MTS.

ALTAI MTS.

GOBI DESERT

Ebinur Hu
Karamay

Yining
Kuytun

Dzungaria

Dalardzadgad

Baotou
Beijing
Tangshan
Bo Gulf
Korea Bay

KYRGYZSTAN

Aksu

TIAN SHAN

Urumqi
Hami
Turfan Depression

Shizuishan

MU US DESERT

Tianjin
Weihai
Yantai
YELLOW SEA
Qingdao
Zibo

Kashi

Bosten Lake

TAKLIMAKAN DESERT

Yumen

ALTUN SHAN

QILIAN SHAN

Yinchuan
Shijiazhuang
Jinan

Cheju I.

Hotan

KARAKORAM

Mt. K2

KUNLUN SHAN

Xining
Lanzhou
Huang He
Xuzhou
Zhengzhou

Qinghai Lake
Huang He

C H I N A

Xi'an

Hongze Lake
Nantong
EAST CHINA SEA

INDIA

HIMALAYA

NEPAL

PLATEAU OF TIBET

BAYAN HAR SHAN

TANGGULA SHAN

Siling Lake

Tangra Lake
Nam Lake
Lhasa

Mt. Everest 8,848 m
Xigaze

BHUTAN

Qamdo

Chengdu
Leshan

SICHUAN BASIN

Chang Jiang

Yichang

Wuhan
Macheng

Dongting Lake

Chongqing
Luzhou

DALOU SHAN

Changsha

Hengyang

NAN LING MTS.

Chao Lake
Hangzhou

Nanjing
Shanghai
Linhai

Poyang Lake
Nanchang
Wenzhou

Fuzhou

Ningbo

Taiwan Strait

Zhangzhou
Taipei
TAIWAN

SALWEEN

AILAO MTS.

MEKONG

MYANMAR (Burma)

LAOS

Xiaguan
Kunming
Gejiu

Guiyang

Liuzhou
Xi Jiang
Guangzhou

Xiamen
Shantou
Kaohsiung

Hong Kong
MACAO

Nanning

VIETNAM

Pingxiang
Zhanjiang

Gulf of Tongkin

Haikou

Hainan

CHINA

HONG KONG

TAIWAN

▶ **Pagoda roofs**
Pagodas are graceful towers with many storeys. The pagoda design came into China from India, along with the Buddhist faith, over 1,500 years ago.

86

CHINA AND ITS NEIGHBOURS

The People's Republic of China is the world's third biggest nation, occupying an area about the size of western Europe. For the last 50 years the southern Chinese island of Taiwan has had its own government. To the north is Mongolia, and in the northeast are North and South Korea.

China is the giant of the Far East, with a population of 1,236,700,000 – the largest in the world. Most Chinese live in the eastern half of the country. This is crossed to the north by the Huang He or Yellow River, which takes its name from the thick mud which colours its waters. The river winds through a rich soil called loess, which has been blown here from deserts to the north. Northern China has bitterly cold winters and warm summers. It produces wheat and fruit, and is rich in resources such as coal and timber. Many large cities are in the north, including the capital, Beijing. Beijing is growing rapidly into a modern city of high-rise buildings and highways. However it still contains many ancient buildings, such as the Imperial Palace, known as the Forbidden City, and the Temple of Heaven, or Tiantan.

Central China is crossed by the world's third longest river, the Chang Jiang (sometimes called the Yangze). It runs from the western mountains through the province of Sechuan. After passing through steep gorges and a series of dams, it spills across the fertile plains of the east. The great port of Shanghai, by the East China Sea, lies on a tributary of the Chang Jiang.

Southern China includes the island of Hainan, sunny Yunnan province, misty lakes and rivers, the great cities of Guangzhou and Hong Kong. The latter, a centre of international business, was a British colony until 1997.

◀ *Water and sky*
Aberdeen, on the southern side of Hong Kong's Victoria Island, takes in both towering skyscrapers and sampans, small boats used as floating homes.

Standard Chinese is spoken by more people than any other language in the world, and the southern dialect of Cantonese is also widely spoken.

Southern China's warm, humid climate is ideal for growing rice, which is China's staple crop. The coast of the South China Sea is sometimes battered by seasonal tropical storms called typhoons.

China is ringed by high mountains and fierce deserts. The remote west includes areas such as Xinjiang and Tibet, which at times in its history has been an independent country. Nine out of ten Chinese belong to the Han people, but there are over 50 other 'minority' peoples, distinguished by their own customs, languages or religions.

The Chinese have been influenced by various beliefs. Confucianism is a belief in social order and respect for one's ancestors. Daoism is based upon a belief in harmony and nature. Buddhism first came to China from India. The three beliefs became mingled over the ages.

Chinese civilization grew up over 5,000 years ago. China became a united empire in 221BC, and rule by emperors continued until 1911. The Chinese were great poets, artists and technical innovators. They invented paper, printing, gunpowder and the manufacture of silk. They produced the world's finest pottery, known as porcelain – or 'china'.

In the 1930s and 40s China saw invasion by the Japanese and a bitter civil war between Communists and Nationalists. The Japanese were defeated and the Communists came to power

▲ *Planting rice, South Korea*
Women plant out rice seedlings in paddy fields near Andong, in central South Korea. Rice is the staple diet of the Far East.

FAR EASTERN FOODS
Chinese cooking is said to be
amongst the best in the world. It
varies greatly from one region to
another. Favourite dishes include
rice, noodles and dumplings, duck
and pork, fish, fresh green
vegetables and soya bean
curd. Some regions like
hot and peppery
tastes, with chilis and
peanuts.

◄Getting around
Tram, taxi, rail or
ferry are all travel
options in Hong
Kong, the former
British colony which returned
to Chinese rule in 1997.

peoples is divided between China,
the Russian Federation and the
independent republic of
Mongolia. This is a large but
sparsely populated country, with
empty, rolling grasslands and
desert. Many of its people are
nomads, living by herding
sheep and camels. Some
still live in round tents
called gers or yurts. In
the Middle Ages
Mongol horsemen
conquered China to the
south and also invaded
large areas of Central Asia
and Eastern Europe.

The Korean peninsula is the
centre of another ancient
civilisation. In 1950-53 the
country was torn apart by a bitter
war between the communist
world and the west. Korea
became two separate, hostile
countries. North Korea remained
communist, while South Korea
became a major centre of business
and manufacture.

in 1949. The
Nationalists fled to the
island of Taiwan, where
they set up a rival
government. Taiwan
today is an international
centre of business and
manufacture. Mainland
China is still ruled by the
Communist Party, but it
now promotes big business
rather than following
Communist policies.

For hundreds of years Chinese
people have settled overseas and
brought their culture to other
parts of the world. There are
large Chinese communities in
Southeast Asia, North America
and Western Europe. Dragon
dancers may be seen celebrating
Chinese New Year on the streets
of San Francisco, London or
Singapore.

The homeland of the Mongol

▼ The Great Wall of China
This wall defended the ancient Chinese
empire against northern invaders.
Thousands of kilometres of the wall may
still be seen today.

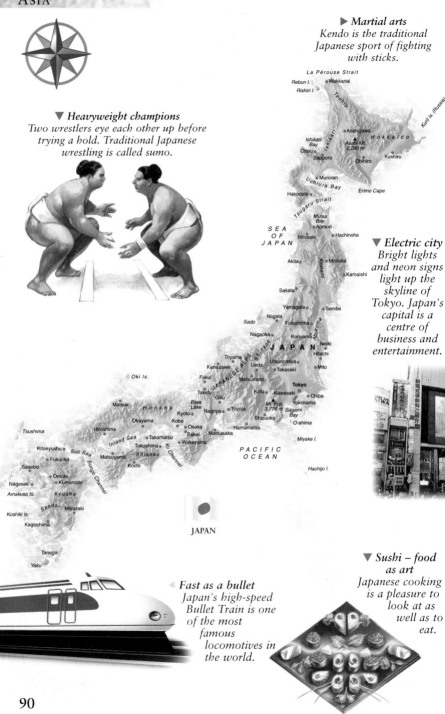

▶ Martial arts
Kendo is the traditional
Japanese sport of fighting
with sticks.

▼ Heavyweight champions
Two wrestlers eye each other up before
trying a hold. Traditional Japanese
wrestling is called sumo.

▼ Electric city
Bright lights
and neon signs
light up the
skyline of
Tokyo. Japan's
capital is a
centre of
business and
entertainment.

La Pérouse Strait
Rebun I. • Wakkanai
Rishiri I.
Kuril Is. (Russia)
Asanigawa
Ishikari Hokkaido
Bay   Asahi Mt.
Otaru   2,290 m
Sapporo Obihiro Kushiro
Uchiura Bay
Muroran
Hakodate Erimo Cape
Tsugaru Strait
Mutsa
Bay
Aomori
SEA   Hirosaki Hachinohe
OF
JAPAN Akita Morioka
Kamaishi
Sakata
Yamagata Sendai
Sado Niigata
Nagaoka Fukushima
Koriyama Iwaki
J A P A N Hitachi
Toyama Utsunomiya Mito
Kanazawa Ueda Takasaki
Oki Is. Fukui Matsumoto
Takefu Kofu Kawasaki Chiba
Matsue Gifu Tokyo
Honshu Kyoto Nagoya Toyota Yokohama
Okayama Kobe Mt. Fuji Sagami
Biwa   Osaka 3,776 m Bay
Lake   Sakai Shizuoka O-shima
Tsushima Hiroshima Matsusaka
Takamatsu Hamamatsu
Kitakyushu Tokushima Wakayama Miyake I.
Suo Sea Matsuyama Shikoku
Fukuoka Kochi PACIFIC
Sasebo Bungo Channel OCEAN
Omuta
Nagasaki Kumamoto Hachijo I.
Amakusa Is. Kyushu
Koshiki Is. Sendai Miyazaki
Kagoshima

JAPAN

Tanega
Yaku

Fast as a bullet
Japan's high-speed
Bullet Train is one
of the most
famous
locomotives in
the world.

**▼ Sushi – food
as art**
Japanese cooking
is a pleasure to
look at as
well as to
eat.

90

JAPAN

A long string of over 3,000 islands makes up the country of Japan. The islands lie off the eastern coast of Asia, between the Sea of Japan and the open waters of the Pacific Ocean. The four largest ones are called Kyushu, Shikoku, Honshu and Hokkaido.

Lying on the rim of the Pacific Ocean, Japan lies in one of the world's danger zones for earthquakes and volcanic eruptions. Inland, the islands are mostly forested and mountainous, so most of the agricultural regions, as well as the cities, are to be found on the flat lands around the coast.

Japan is famous for its spring blossoms, and much of the country has a mild climate. However, northern winters can be cold and very snowy, while southern islands extend towards the warmth of the tropics.

Japan grows rice, fruit, vegetables and tea. It has a big fishing fleet and there is a huge market for the catch. Japan has few natural resources but has become one of the world's leading industrial countries, selling cars and electrical goods around the world. The capital city, Tokyo, is on the island of Honshu. Its buildings have spread out to merge with those of Yokohama, forming one of the largest town areas of the world. Over three-quarters of all Japanese are city-dwellers.

Japan is famous for its ancient buildings as well as for its modern banks and offices. They include temples and shrines of the Buddhist and Shinto religions, as well as tall castles. Japan's history was made by emperors with splendid courts, by armoured knights called samurai and by great artists and architects. Its craft workers were masters of design, producing beautiful pottery. During the Second World War, between 1940 and 1945, Japan invaded a large area of the Far East and fought against the Allies. In 1945 terrible atomic bombs dropped on the cities of Hiroshima and Nagasaki brought this war to an end.

Nearly all the people of Japan are Japanese, although a small number in the north are descended from the islands' first inhabitants, a people called the Ainu. Japan still has an emperor, but today real power lies with its democratic parliament.

MYANMAR
(BURMA)

LAOS

THAILAND

CAMBODIA

PHILIPPINES

BRUNEI

VIETNAM

SINGAPORE

MALAYSIA

INDONESIA

SOUTH EAST ASIA

The tropical lands of southeast Asia lie between the Indian and Pacific Oceans. The mainland tapers into a long, thin peninsula, which breaks up into a chain of volcanic islands. Thailand, Laos, Cambodia and Vietnam occupy the north of the region. Malaysia, Singapore, Brunei and Indonesia occupy the south, while the Philippines lie in the east.

Southeast Asia is home to a fascinating mixture of hundreds of different peoples. There are the Thais, the Hmong, Khmer, Cham, Lao, Annamese, Chinese, Indians, Dayaks, Iban, Toradja, Moluccans, Filipinos, all with their own languages and cultures. Religions include Buddhism, Hinduism, Islam and Christianity. Many Southeast Asians have settled overseas, in the Netherlands, Australia and North America. Thai and Malaysian cooking has become popular around the world.

Much of the southeast Asian mainland is occupied by Thailand. This country, once known as Siam, descends from the mountains along the border with Myanmar (Burma) to the network of rivers which flow into the Gulf of Thailand. A thin sliver of territory stretches southwards down the Isthmus of Kra to the Malaysian border. The land is green with teak forests and rice paddies. Tourists visit Thailand to see its beautiful beaches and its

◀ *Whatever the weather*
Broad-brimmed, cone-shaped straw hats are worn by field workers in many parts of Southeast Asia. They keep off both the hot sun and the monsoon rains.

ancient Buddhist temples. Thailand is a kingdom and was the only nation in the region to avoid foreign rule in the 1800s and 1900s.

The three countries to the east, Cambodia, Laos and Vietnam, all came under French rule at that time and were known as Indo-China. They too have tropical forests, highland regions and flooded rice paddies. They are linked by the Mekong, a great river which flows from China right across the region into southern Vietnam. These are beautiful countries with ancient cultures and splendid Buddhist temples.

Sadly, they have all seen terrible fighting in the last 60 years. This included

APUA
NEW
UINEA

◀ **Green terraces, Thailand**
Rice has been grown on the terraced hillsides of Southeast Asia for thousands of years. They are flooded by irrigation channels.

Japanese invasion in the 1940s, a French bid to take the region back under its rule in the 1950s, the terrible Vietnam War of the 1960s and 70s, in which the United States failed to defeat the Vietnamese Communists, and a brutal civil war in Cambodia in the 1970s and 80s. Today these nations are looking forward to more peaceful times.

Malaysia takes up the southern part of the long Southeast Asian peninsula, but also includes the regions of Sarawak and Sabah on the island of Borneo. The country produces rice, rubber and oil. Its rainforests are home to lush plants and strange animals such as the orang-utan, a giant ape. Like

other countries in the region the forests have been devastated by logging over the years, and by fires which have caused widespread air pollution. The Malaysian capital, Kuala Lumpur, is a centre of international business, which boasts the world's highest office buildings, the twin 451.9 metre-high Petronas Towers.

Another world business centre is Singapore, built on islands across the Johor Strait.

▶ *Peace of the spirit*
Thailand is a Buddhist country and has many sacred sites and statues. There are over 27,000 Buddhist temples.

▶ *A floating market*
Vegetables and fruit are traded directly from small boats on this waterway near Bangkok.

▼ **City by the sea**
Singapore is a great centre of trade. Its population of nearly 3 million includes people of Chinese, Malay, Tamil and European descent.

Singapore was ruled by Britain from 1858 until 1959. Much of the state's territory is now taken up by the modern buildings of Singapore City, where nearly all the population lives. In the 1960s Singapore was briefly united with Malaysia, but it broke away to become an independent state.

The rapid growth of economic development in countries such as Singapore and Malaysia in the 1980s gave them the nickname of 'Asian tigers'. However, by the end of the 1990s all Far Eastern economies seemed to face a less certain future.

The Sultanate of Brunei is a small independent nation on the north coast of Borneo. Oil wealth has made its ruler the richest man in the world. Much of the country is covered in tropical forest, which is being damaged by illegal logging. Plantations produce bananas and rubber.

Indonesia, formerly ruled by the Dutch, is a nation of islands – many thousands of them. The largest are Sumatra, Java, southern Borneo, Sulawesi and western New Guinea, which is called Irian Jaya. The forested islands lie on the Pacific rim, notorious for it violent volcanoes. The destruction of the island of Krakatoa in 1883 was the worst eruption in the world's recorded history. The Indonesian population today numbers over 204 million, and is the world's

DRAGONS AND BUTTERFLIES

The volcanic islands and tropical rainforests of Southeast Asia support many weird and wonderful animals. Many are rare or threatened by the destruction of the forests where they live. The komodo dragon of Indonesia is the world's biggest lizard. The smallest mammal lives in Thailand – a bat which is the size of a bumblebee. There are other spectacular species like giant butterflies, sea snakes and flying frogs.

largest Islamic nation. Its government is under increasing pressure to improve its record on human rights and democracy, especially on the island of East Timor, which it occupied in 1975, and in Irian Jaya. The islands produce rice, rubber, coffee, oil and natural gas. The beautiful island of Bali, with its unique form of Hinduism, attracts tourists from all over the world. Indonesia is famous for its patterned textiles, dyed by methods known known as batik and ikat.

Finally we travel eastwards to the Philippines, on the edge of the open Pacific Ocean. This maze of 7,000 small islands was once ruled by Spain and later by the United States. It became independent in 1946. The Philippines produce rice, timber, electrical goods and garments. Its people are mostly Roman Catholic.

AFRICA

TUNISIA

EGYPT

▶ **The mysterious Sphinx**
This great stone statue stares across the desert sands at Giza, near Cairo. It is over 4,500 years old.

ALGERIA

LIBYA

ERITREA

MOROCCO

DJIBOUTI

SUDAN

CAMEROON

Map

Strait of Gibraltar
Madeira
Tétouan
Oran
Algiers
Annaba
Tunis
Casablanca
Oujda
Constantine
Rabat
MOROCCO
Sfax
TUNISIA
Marrakech
Agadir
ATLAS MOUNTAINS
ATLAS MTS.
Béchar
Ghardaia
Tripoli
Misurata
Benghazi
Gulf of Sirte
Darnah
Port S
Ifni
CANARY
ISLANDS
Ghadamis
Alexandria
**Western
Sahara**
Las Palmas
Tindouf
A L G E R I A
Adrar
In Salah
L I B Y A
QATTARA
DEPRESSION
Cairo
Asyût
Dakhla
S   A   H   A   R   A
AHAGGAR MTS.
Tahat
2,918 m
LIBYAN DESERT
E G Y P T
Lake
Nasser
Cape
Blanc
MAURITANIA
TIBESTI
MTS.
Emi Koussi
3,415 m ▲
Nu
De
Mere
Nile
CAPE VERDE
ISLANDS
Nouakchott
M A L I
A I R
M T S.
Faya-Largeau
Praia
Dakar
Kaédi
Timbuktu
N I G E R
C H A D
S U D A N
Omd
Sénégal
Niger
BODÉLÉ
DEPRESSION
SENEGAL
Banjul
Kayes
Ségou
Niamey
Zinder
Lake
Chad
Abéché
El Obeid
Khartou
Bissau
GAMBIA
Bamako
Ouagadougou
Kano
Maiduguri
N'Djamena
Jabal Marrah
3,088
K
**GUINEA-
BISSAU**
GUINEA
Conakry
Kankan
BURKINA FASO
Zaria
Kaduna
Chari
Freetown
**IVORY
COAST**
Tamale
Niger
Benue
Yola
Garoua
Sarh
SUDD
**SIERRA
LEONE**
Man
Bouaké
Lake
Volta
Porto-
Novo
Abuja
Ibadan
NIGERIA
Benin City
Monrovia
Yamoussoukro
Kumasi
Lagos
LIBERIA
Greenville
Abidjan
GHANA
Accra
Lomé
Port Harcourt
White
Cape Palmas
Benin City
CAMEROON
CENTRAL AFRICAN
REPUBLIC
Malabo
Yaoundé
Bioko
Douala
EQUATORIAL GUINEA
U

CAPE VERDE

TOGO

MAURITANIA

CHAD

ETHIO

NIGERIA

GUINEA-BISSAU

GUINEA

IVORY COAST

GHANA

BEN

MALI

SIERRA LEONE

LIBERIA

BURKINA FASO

SENEGAL

▶ **Roman Tunisia**
In ancient times the North African coast was settled by Greeks, Carthaginians and Romans. This is the Roman coliseum at El Jem, in Tunisia.

GAMBIA

NORTH AND WEST AFRICA

The Sahara is the world's biggest desert. This wilderness of sand, gravel and rock swelters under a burning sun. To the north it is fringed by the green lands of the Mediterranean. To the south it gives way to dusty grasslands, the humid Guinea coast, the swamps of southern Sudan and the mountains of Ethiopia.

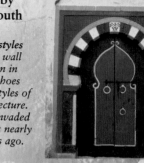

▶ Arabic styles
A modern wall decoration in Tunisia echoes traditional styles of Arab architecture. The Arabs invaded North Africa nearly 1,400 years ago.

The countries of Morocco, Algeria and Tunisia are sometimes known as the Maghreb, the 'far west' of the Arab world. They are also home to the Berber peoples. Their coastal lands enjoy a mild climate, and are farmed for wheat, olives, oranges and vegetables. Southwards the land rises to the ranges of the Atlas mountains, whose valleys are grazed by goats and sheep.

In the south of these countries are the shifting sands of the Sahara, crossed by ancient trading routes. Peoples such as the Tuareg cross the desert's ancient trading routes by camel. They camp at oases, where water supplies make it possible to grow dates and figs. The state of Western Sahara, rich in phosphates, is claimed by Morocco.

Africa's northeastern countries, Libya and Egypt, are also Arab lands. Their deserts are scorched dry, but in the east they are crossed by the Nile, the world's longest river. Its banks provide a narrow, fertile strip and a green delta region on the Mediterranean coast. Africa's first great civilization grew up along the Nile over 5,000 years ago. Egypt's capital, Cairo, is the biggest city in Africa. Cotton and textiles are important exports.

Branches of the Nile also cross through the lands to the

◄ Bridge over the Nile
Cairo, the capital of Egypt, lies on the River Nile. Egypt has always depended on this great waterway for its survival.

south of Egypt. Sudan is Africa's largest country, with deserts in the north, green mountains in the west and a vast wetland region called the Sudd in the south. While the north of the country lies within the Arab world, the south is home to a wide variety of Black African farming and cattle herding peoples,

A camel's eye view
The spectacular pyramids of Giza mark royal tombs, dating back to the early days of ancient Egypt. Camels were not introduced into Egypt until much later.

such as the Dinka and Shilluk. Ethiopia is a mountainous land which becomes desert in the east. It grows grain crops such as maize, sorghum and teff, as well as coffee and sugar cane. Two small countries, Eritrea and Djibouti, share its Red Sea coastline.

The lands to the south of the Sahara are known as the Sahel countries. They include Mauritania, Mali, Burkina Faso, Niger and Chad. Desert sands are blown southwards by seasonal winds into the Sahel's dry grasslands, which are grazed by cattle and goats. This whole belt of Africa suffers greatly from drought and famine is common. The people are often desperately poor.

Further south, the climate becomes more moist and the soil richer. West Africa is a great bulge of land ranged around the Gulf of Guinea, crossed by branches of the River Burkina or Volta, and by the mighty River Niger. It includes plateaus and rolling hill country, descending to tropical forest and swamps along the humid, palm-fringed coast. The region has rich natural resources, such as oil and diamonds, but most of the people have remained poor. Crops include cocoa, rubber, palm-oil, peanuts and cotton.

The countries of the west are the Cape Verde Islands, Senegal and Gambia, Guinea and Guinea-Bissau, Sierra Leone and Liberia. The central gulf states are Côte d'Ivoire, Ghana, Togo, Benin and Nigeria, whose population of over 107 million is the biggest in Africa.

DESERT SURVIVORS

The Sahara is one of the most inhospitable regions on Earth, but many creatures have learned how to survive in the desert. They include deadly scorpions (right), a type of antelope called the addax and the fennec, a fox whose big ears help it to lose heat. The sandgrouse flies to oases where it traps drops of water in its feathers.

▲ *Ethiopian bread*
Injera is a flat, doughy bread which is eaten in Ethiopia. It is used to mop up meat and vegetable stews.

The eastern gulf states, around the Bight of Biafra, take in Cameroon, Equatorial Guinea and the offshore islands of São Tomé and Príncipe.

Islam is the religion of the Saharan countries, but the southern regions of West Africa and southern Sudan are Christian. The Ethiopian Church is over 1,600 years old. In many areas, traditional African beliefs in spirits are still popular.

Hundreds of different peoples live in the Sahel and West African countries, including the Malinke, Ewe, Kabre, Kulani, Kanuri, Ibo and Yoruba. In ancient times there were powerful empires in both Ethiopia and West Africa. Ethiopia did remain independent, but most of the region suffered raids by slave traders, foreign invasion and colonial rule. Colonial languages including English, French and Portuguese may still be heard. All the countries of the region are now independent.

◄ Fishing in Lake Malawi
Fishermen set up a ring of nets. This lake, 5760 kilometres long, is a drowned section of the Great Rift Valley.

ANGOLA

BOTSWANA

RWANDA

SOMALIA

ZIMBABWE

BURUNDI

ZAMBIA

MOZAMBIQUE

SEYCHELLES

CENTRAL AFRICAN REPUBLIC

MALAWI

CONGO

UGANDA

KENYA

GABON

SÃO TOMÉ & PRÍNCIPE

MAURITIUS

SEYCHELLES

NAMIBIA

MADAGASCAR

SOUTH AFRICA

LESOTHO

► Traditional lives
The masai people live on the high, dry grasslands of souther Kenya and northern Tanzania, where the raise cattle.

CENTRAL, EASTERN AND SOUTHERN AFRICA

The southern half of the African continent includes hot and humid forests around the Equator, grasslands such as the East African savannah and the South African veldt, burning deserts and high mountains. Volcanoes and lakes mark the course of the Great Rift Valley, a deep crack in the Earth's surface. Offshore, coral islands and reefs stretch eastwards into the Indian Ocean.

The Central African Republic lies at the heart of the continent, a small country with grassy highlands in the north and tropical forests in the southwest. The River Ubangi flows south into the River Congo, which divides the small country of Congo from its large southern neighbour, the Democratic Republic of the Congo (known as Zaïre from 1971 to 1997). The two Congolese capitals, Brazzaville and Kinshasa, lie on either side of the river. The country of Gabon stretches from the Congo border to the Atlantic Ocean. The Equator runs through these steamy lands of dense rainforest, which are home to many different peoples, including Pygmies. Many people travel by riverboat or canoe, especially when roads are washed away by the rains. In the east are the volcanic mountains of the Ruwenzori range. The Democratic Republic of the Congo has rich mineral resources including diamonds, but over the ages its wealth has been seized by colonial powers and corrupt rulers, leaving most people as poor farmers. The pop music of the region is listened to over a wide area of Africa.

On the Democratic Republic's eastern borders, the tiny countries of Rwanda and Burundi cling to steep slopes where bananas, maize and beans are grown.

These two countries have seen long years of conflict between the Hutu and Tutsi peoples who live there.

The course of Africa's Great Rift Valley is marked by deep lakes and volcanoes, stretching from Ethiopia to Malawi. Fossil remains of humans' earliest ancestors have been found in its rocky gorges. The region of East Africa stretches from the red, fertile farmland of Uganda, between Lake Albert and Lake Victoria, to the blue waters of the Indian Ocean. Somalia occupies the arid Horn of Africa, but to the south are the grassy plains of Kenya and Tanzania, dotted with acacia trees and patches of scrub. Beneath the snow-capped slopes of Mount Kilimanjaro, great herds of elephant, zebra and wildebeeste still roam. East African farms produce sisal, vegetables, coffee, tea and fruit,

▼ *The African elephant*
The world's biggest land mammal is found in many parts of Eastern and Southern Africa, where it is protected within national parks.

▶ *The smoke that thunders...*
That is one of the local names for the Victoria Falls, between Zimbabwe and Zambia. Three cascades are created where the bed of the River Zambezi drops by 122 metres.

◀ *Snap!*
The Nile crocodile is found through most of Africa. It grows into a ferocious adult, which can be well over 6 metres long. Crocodiles are also raised on special farms, for their hide.

and raise cattle. The island of Zanzibar is famous for its spices. Tourism is a growing industry. Hundreds of different African peoples live in East Africa, as well as some of European, Arab and Indian descent. The Swahili language is understood over a large part of the region. Some East Africans live very traditional lives, while others work in modern cities such as Nairobi, Mombasa or Dar-es-Salaam.

▼ Masai ornament
Beaded collars and earrings are the traditional dress of Masai women, who live across the Kenyan–Tanzanian border.

PARCHED EARTH

Between 50 and 150 kilometres across, the Namib desert follows the southwest African coast for over 1,200 kilometres. Rain hardly ever falls here, even though the air is often filled with fog where cold ocean currents meet the warm landmass.

South of Tanzania, beautiful tropical lands are crossed by the River Zambezi. The nations of Malawi, Mozambique, Zimbabwe and Zambia include fertile farmlands growing tobacco, vegetables and maize. There are also rich deposits of copper and other minerals. Botswana, in central Southern Africa, is largely given over to cattle ranching. It includes the Kalahari desert, home of the San people, and the great Okavango swamp. Southwestern nations include Angola and Namibia, where the harshness of the Namib desert resulted in its Atlantic region once being called the Skeleton Coast.

The Republic of South Africa is the continent's richest and most powerful country. It includes high grasslands and plateaus known as veld, the Drakensberg mountain range, and great cities such as Cape Town and Johannesburg. From 1950 to 1994 South Africa was divided by a racist policy called apartheid, which kept the Black majority from power. The mild climate of the south is ideal for growing grape vines and fruit. The country's wealth derives from its mineral resources, which include gold and diamonds. The population includes Zulus, Xhosa, Sotho, Afrikaners (the descendants of Dutch settlers) and Asians. South Africa's borders surround the small independent countries of Lesotho and Swaziland. Out in the Indian Ocean are the island nations of the Comoros, the Seychelles, Mauritius and Africa's largest island, Madagascar.

▲ Sorghum crop, Zimbabwe
Hardy sorghum is a crop well adapted to the heat and occasional droughts of southeast African farms.

103

▶ *Tracking the skies*
Tidbinbilla Deep Space
Tracking Station, near
Canberra, is one of the three
most powerful receivers of
space signals in the world.

Torres Strait
C. York
Melville I.
Bathurst I.
Darwin
C. Arnhem
Gulf of
Carpentaria
CAPE
YORK
PENINSULA
Joseph
Bonaparte
Gulf
Bonaparte
Archipelago
Daly
Arnhem Land
Roper
Groote
Eylandt
Wellesley Is.
Mitchell
Gilbert
GREAT BARRIER REEF
Cairns
KIMBERLEY
PLATEAU
Fitzroy
Broome
NORTHERN
TERRITORY
BARKLY TABLELAND
Mount Isa
Norman
Flinders
Townsville
Proserpine
Mackay
Eighty Mile Beach
Port Hedland
De Grey
Barrow I.
Fortescue
Mt. Bruce
Ashburton
GREAT
SANDY
DESERT
Georgina
QUEENSLAND
C. Townse
Rockha
Bund
GIBSON
DESERT
MACDONNELL RANGES
Alice Springs
Uluru (Ayers Rock)
867m
SIMPSON
DESERT
Diamantina
Thomson
Barcoo
Belyando
GREAT DIVIDING RANGE
Lake
Macleod
Carnarvon
Dirk
Hartog I.
Murchison
WESTERN AUSTRALIA
Finke
MUSGRAVE RANGES
Alberga
L. Eyre
Cooper Creek
Warrego
Culgoa
Bris
Toowoomba
Gold Ce
Geraldton
Laverton
GREAT
VICTORIA
DESERT
SOUTH AUSTRALIA
Barwon
NULLARBOR PLAIN
L. Everard
L. Gairdner
L. Torrens
FLINDERS RANGE
Broken Hill
Darling
NEW SOUTH WALES
H
Maitla
Perth
Fremantle
Kalgoorlie-Boulder
Great Australian Bight
Lachlan
Newc
Sydne
Wollongo
C. Naturaliste
Bunbury
C. Leeuwin
Albany
Archipelago of the
Recherche
Port Lincoln
Spencer Gulf
Adelaide
Mildura
Wagga Wagga
Murray
Canberra AUSTRALIAN
CAPITAL
TERRITORY
Kangaroo I.
VICTORIA
Bendigo
Ballarat
Mt. Kosciusko
2,228m
C. Howe
Mount
Gambier
Geelong
Melbourne
C. Otway
Wilson's Promontory
TASM.
SEA
King I.
Bass Strait
Flinders I.
Cape Barren I.
Burnie
Davenport
Launceston
Queenstown
TASMANIA
Hobart
South East C.

▶ *City on the harbour*
Sydney is Australia's biggest
city. Its beautiful harbour has
the world's widest long-span
bridge and an opera house
whose roofs look like billowing
sails.

AUSTRALIA

This island is so huge that it is considered to be a landmass in its own right. Lying at the bottom of the world, between the Indian and Pacific Oceans, it is fringed to the east by the world's longest stretch of coral, the Great Barrier Reef. It includes several offshore islands, the biggest of which is Tasmania, across Bass Strait.

The interior of Australia is a wilderness like no other. Baked by intense heat, it is a very ancient land of glowing rocks and empty desert, of cracked earth and salt lakes. These are surrounded by a variety of landscapes, from rolling grasslands grazed by huge herds of sheep and cattle, to the tropical forests of the northeast where crocodiles lurk in muddy creeks, to southern scrubland and eucalyptus woods.

The Great Dividing Range runs parallel with the Pacific Coast, reaching 2,228 metres above sea level at Mount Kosciusko, in the Snowy Mountains. The Murray River rises here and flows 2,560

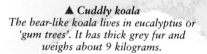

▲ *Cuddly koala*
The bear-like koala lives in eucalyptus or 'gum trees'. It has thick grey fur and weighs about 9 kilograms.

kilometres to Encounter Bay, joined on the way by its tributaries, the Lachlan, Murrumbidgee, Goulburn and Darling rivers.

The Australian coastline is indented by two huge bays, the Great Australian Bight, below the vast southern flatlands of the Nullarbor Plain, and in the north, the Gulf of Carpentaria, which divides Cape York Peninsula from Arnhem Land. The island of Tasmania includes mountains, temperate

rainforests and wild coastlines.

Australia has many animals and birds seen nowhere else on earth. They include the duck-billed platypus (an egg-laying river mammal), kangaroos and wallabies, who keep their babies in a pouch, wombats, deadly snakes and spiders, frilled lizards and large flightless birds called emus.

Australia's cities turn their backs on the remote interior, which is known as the 'Outback'. Instead, they look outwards to blue seas, where ocean breakers pound sandy beaches. The two biggest cities are Sydney and Melbourne, both in the southeast of the country. They are old rivals in business and trade. Brisbane is the chief city of the east, Adelaide

of the south, and Perth of the west. The city of Canberra, surrounded by Australian Capital Territory (ACT), is a purpose-built capital centred on the federal parliament buildings.

Australia is divided into separate states which have their own regional governments. Tropical Queensland grows sugar cane, pineapples and bananas. New South Wales and Victoria produce the wool, meat and dairy products which first brought prosperity to Australia. These two states include the chief centres of business, finance and

▲ **Laughing Kookaburra**
This bird is the largest of the kingfishers. Its cackling call sounds just like laughter.

◀ **Flinders Street**
This fine old railway station, just to the north of the Yarra River, links central Melbourne with its sprawling suburbs.

communications. Southern Australia grows grapes and produces excellent wines. Tasmania has a timber industry, often challenged by conservation campaigners. It also raises livestock and grows apples and pears. Minerals are important in Western Australia and the remote Northern Territory. Tourism is a growing industry throughout Australia. Popular sports include Australian Rules football, rugby football, cricket and tennis.

Descendants of the first Australians are called Aborigines. Their ancestors entered the land across the Torres Strait from perhaps 50,000 years ago. They became experts at surviving in harsh environments and were skilled hunters with spear and boomerang. Some groups were nomadic while others were settled. A rich body of myths and legends grew up amongst the Aborigines, who still look back to a magical 'Dreamtime'.

In the 1600s Dutch navigators began to explore the Australian coast. In 1770 the English sea captain James Cook claimed New South Wales for Great Britain. The first colonists were prisoners sent out from Britain, but soon many other British people arrived to farm or search for gold. The Aborigines were persecuted and murdered and their lands were stolen. They have faced a long struggle to regain their lands and to achieve civil rights.

Today's Australians include people of many different

ABORIGINAL ART

Australia has a lively arts scene and its galleries include many paintings by Aborigines. These are often inspired by ancient myths and sacred landscapes, showing bold patterns and pictures of animals and birds. Traditional paintings were often of vegetable pigments on bark, but modern Aboriginal artists may also use all kinds of other media such as acrylic paint.

backgrounds and cultures. There are Irish, Italians, Greeks, Dutch, Scandinavians, Lebanese, Vietnamese, Thais and Indians in addition to the Australians of Aboriginal and British descent. Australia has retained close cultural links with Great Britain, but is considering breaking its historical ties with the British monarchy to become a republic. It increasingly sees itself as a major economic power of the Pacific Rim.

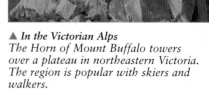

▲ *In the Victorian Alps*
The Horn of Mount Buffalo towers over a plateau in northeastern Victoria. The region is popular with skiers and walkers.

107

North Cape

Whangerei

Gt. Barrier Island

Auckland •Manukau

Bay of
Plenty

East Cape

Hamilton

Waikato

Rotorua

NORTH
ISLAND

L. Taupo

Gisborne

New Plymouth

Ruapehu
2,797m

Napier

NEW ZEALAND

Wanganui

Hastings

Cape Farewell

Palmerston North

Nelson

Cook Strait

Wellington

Westport

Blenheim

Greymouth

SOUTHERN ALPS

SOUTH
ISLAND

Mt.Cook 3,764m

Canterbury
Plains

Christchurch

Timaru

Clutha

Dunedin

Foveaux Strait

Invercargill

Stewart Island

▶ *Tropical cascade*
A waterfall drops through the lush New Guinea
forest. Giant butterflies and birds of paradise
flourish in the island's humid climate.

▶ *Welcome to Bora Bora*
This is one of the Society Islands in
French Polynesia. The region includes
many volcanic peaks and forested valleys.

NEW ZEALAND AND THE PACIFIC

The Pacific Ocean is the largest in the world, covering about one third of the world's surface. It gives its name to Oceania, the group of lands which includes Australia, Papua New Guinea, New Zealand and the thousands of tiny islands scattered across the ocean. Another name for this region is Australasia.

▲ *Canoes of the Pacific*
Trobriand Islanders crew a trading canoe.
Canoes are the traditional method of
travel between Pacific islands.

Papua New Guinea (PNG) occupies the eastern half of the island of New Guinea and also includes many smaller islands, such as New Britain, New Ireland and the northern Solomons. The country includes forested hills and remote valleys, the home of hundreds of different peoples speaking many languages. The highest point in all Oceania is Mount Wilhelm, 4,509 metres above sea level. PNG is rich in copper and exports coffee, tea and rubber.

New Zealand lies about 1,900 kilometres to the southeast of Australia. It is a group of islands, of which the two largest, North and South, are divided by Cook Strait. The islands were settled over a thousand years ago by a Polynesian people called the Maoris. The islands were also discovered by the English explorer James Cook in 1769, and by the 1800s the islands were being colonized by British whalers, farmers, prospectors and traders.

The capital, Wellington, and the largest city, Auckland, are both on North Island. Like many other islands around the Pacific, this is volcanic and has

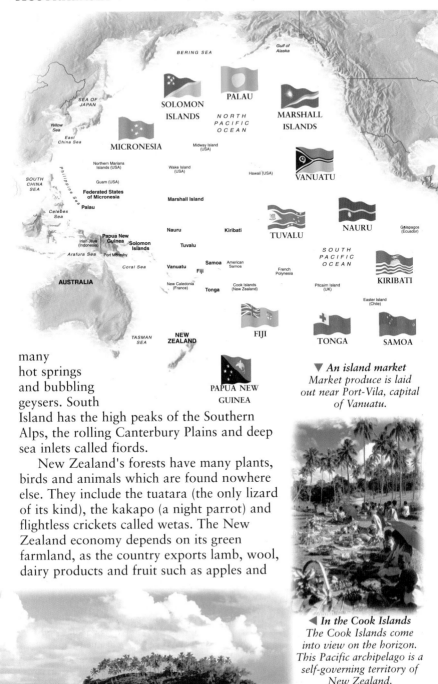

BERING SEA

Gulf of Alaska

SEA OF JAPAN

Yellow Sea

East China Sea

SOLOMON ISLANDS

PALAU

NORTH PACIFIC OCEAN

MARSHALL ISLANDS

MICRONESIA

Midway Island (USA)

Northern Mariana Islands (USA)

Wake Island (USA)

Hawaii (USA)

VANUATU

SOUTH CHINA SEA

Guam (USA)

Federated States of Micronesia

Palau

Marshall Island

Celebes Sea

Nauru

Kiribati

TUVALU

NAURU

Galapagos (Ecuador)

Papua New Guinea

Irian Jaya (Indonesia)

Solomon Islands

Port Moresby

Tuvalu

SOUTH PACIFIC OCEAN

Arafura Sea

AUSTRALIA

Coral Sea

Vanuatu

New Caledonia (France)

Samoa

Fiji

American Samoa

Tonga

French Polynesia

Cook Islands (New Zealand)

Pitcairn Island (UK)

KIRIBATI

Easter Island (Chile)

TASMAN SEA

NEW ZEALAND

FIJI

TONGA

SAMOA

PAPUA NEW GUINEA

▼ *An island market*
Market produce is laid out near Port-Vila, capital of Vanuatu.

many hot springs and bubbling geysers. South Island has the high peaks of the Southern Alps, the rolling Canterbury Plains and deep sea inlets called fiords.

New Zealand's forests have many plants, birds and animals which are found nowhere else. They include the tuatara (the only lizard of its kind), the kakapo (a night parrot) and flightless crickets called wetas. The New Zealand economy depends on its green farmland, as the country exports lamb, wool, dairy products and fruit such as apples and

◀ *In the Cook Islands*
The Cook Islands come into view on the horizon. This Pacific archipelago is a self-governing territory of New Zealand.

▲ *Putting on a show*
Traditionally, many peoples on New Guinea wear body paint, feathers, bones, grass and leaves for special dances and festivals.

pears. Factories produce textiles and plastics and most New Zealanders enjoy a high standard of living.

Many chains of islands dot the vast expanse of the South Pacific. Some are ruled by other nations, but others have joined together to form their own countries. Independent Pacific nations include the Federated States of Micronesia, Palau, the Marshall Islands, Kiribati (pronounced Kiribass), Nauru, the Solomon Islands, Tuvalu, Fiji, Tonga, Vanuatu and Western Samoa.

Most islands of the Pacific are formed from coral or from volcanic rock. Many have villages bordering peaceful blue lagoons and offshore reefs. Coconut palms provide food (often dried and exported as copra), fibre for matting and leaves for roofing. Crops include bananas, vanilla pods, sweet potatoes and taro. Many islanders raise pigs and chickens and catch fish such as tuna. Some islands have mineral

reserves – the island of Nauru has been mined for phosphates on a devastating scale. Cruise liners bring tourists to islands such as Tahiti in French Polynesia.

The peoples of the Pacific fall into three main groups. The Melanesians are the peoples of the west, such as the Solomon Islanders. The Micronesians come from the Marshall and Caroline Islands. The Polynesians have spread right across the ocean from Hawaii to New Zealand. Some islands have also been settled by people of European and Asian descent.

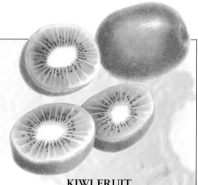

KIWI FRUIT
More kiwi fruit are grown in New Zealand than anywhere else in the world. They are round and soft, with slightly furry skins. Inside they are sweet, green and fleshy. They have become very popular for use in desserts, cakes and salads. Exports of kiwi fruit now bring New Zealand more money than cheese or apples. The success is due to clever marketing. Growers named the fruit after the flightless bird which is the national emblem. 'Kiwi' is also a nickname for any New Zealander.

▲ **Across the ice**
Adélie penguins return to the same breeding grounds each year, shuffling and sliding over the Antarctic ice.

S. Orkney Is

C. Norvegia

S. Shetland Is

Coats Land

Maud Land

Enderby Land

WEDELL SEA

Antarctic Peninsula

Palmer Archipelago

Mac Robertson Land   Cape Darnley

Palmer Land

Berkner I.

PR. CHARLES MTNS.

Alexander I.

Ronne Ice Shelf

PENSACOLA MTNS.

AMERICAN HIGHLAND

Charcot I.

BELLINGHAUSEN SEA

Vinson Massif
▲ 5,410m

South Pole ★

GREATER ANTARCTICA

Queen Mary Land

Ellsworth Land

LESSER ANTARCTICA

TRANSANTARCTIC MTNS.

Knox Coast

Thurston I.

AMUNDSEN SEA

Mt. Kirkpatrick 4,528m ▲

Ross Ice Shelf

Wilkes Land

Siple I.

Marie Byrd Land

Roosevelt I.

Victoria Land

Mt. Erebus 3,794m ▲

ROSS SEA

George V Land

C. Adare

South Magnetic Pole ★

▲ **Southern elephant seal**
This blubbery giant can weigh as much as a truck. It breeds on the bleak islands of the southern oceans, such as South Georgia, Kerguelen and Macquarie.

112

ANTARCTICA

The southernmost point on Earth, the South Pole, lies at the centre of a frozen landmass called Antarctica. This is the coldest and windiest place on Earth, ringed by great sheets of ice.

Nobody has ever settled in Antarctica permanently, but explorers have mapped its icy wilderness and scientists visit special bases to study the climate and geology. Even a few tourists have started to come here, attracted by spectacular sights such as Mount Erebus, an active volcano. The Vinson Massif reaches 4,897 metres above sea level, while the rock of the Bentley Trench is 2,538 metres below sea level – the lowest point on the Earth's crust.

The whole land is buried in deep ice, nearly 5 kilometres thick in places. The seas around the coasts are frozen too, forming great shelves of ice. Massive slabs break off to form icebergs in the southern spring (when the northern part of the Earth is experiencing autumn).

▲ *Ready to dive!*
A humpback whale often slaps the water with its giant tail flukes, making a noise that can be heard several kilometres away.

Antarctica is not part of any country, although several nations claim sections of the territory. Many people believe it should remain under international control and that the rich minerals thought to lie beneath its surface should be left alone. No plants or animals live in the interior, but the southern oceans are rich in sea life, and colonies of penguins and schools of whales may be seen around the coast and islands.

◀ *Weather watch*
A balloon is released from an Antarctic weather station. Antarctica is a good place for scientists to study the state of the ozone layer.

▶ **Modern homes**
*With little timber to
be had for building,
traditional Inuit
homes were made of
turf and stone. Today,
ready-made housing
may be imported and
raised on site.*

Yukon

Bering Strait

**ALASKA
(USA)**

Ambarchik

*CHUKCHI
SEA*

Kolyma

Barrow ● Pt. Barrow

*EAST
SIBERIAN
SEA*

Indigirka

Mackenzie

*BEAUFORT
SEA*

C.Bathurst

New
Siberian
Islands

Lena

**R
U
S
S
I
A**

**C
A
N
A
D
A**

Banks
Island

McClure Strait

Victoria
Island

*ARCTIC
OCEAN*

*LAPTEV
SEA*

Nordvik ●

Queen
Elizabeth
Islands

North Magnetic Pole

Severnaya
Zemlya

Yenisey

★ North Pole

Dikson ●

Ellesmere
Island

Foxe
Basin

Baffin Island

*LINCOLN
SEA*

Franz
Josef
Land

Novaya Zemlya

*KARA
SEA*

Ob'

Baffin
Bay

Davis Strait

**GREENLAND
(DENMARK)**

Svalbard
(Norway)

*BARENTS
SEA*

Pechora

● Godthåb

*GREENLAND
SEA*

North Cape

● Murmansk

Denmark Strait

*NORWEGIAN
SEA*

Archangel ●

ICELAND
● Reykjavik

▶ **Frostbite warning**
*The cold of the Arctic is severe and can
be extremely dangerous. In central
Greenland, temperatures can drop to an
incredible -65°C.*

114

THE ARCTIC

The northernmost point on our planet is called the North Pole. It lies at the centre of the Arctic Ocean, which is permanently covered in a thick ice-cap. Bordering the ocean are the bitterly cold coasts of North America, Europe and Asia.

To reach the North Pole, you either have to travel beneath it in a submarine or cross over the ice cap, battling through fierce blizzards. The countries around this frozen sea take in the American state of Alaska, the maze of islands which make up the Canadian Arctic, Greenland, Norway, Sweden, Finland and the long coastline of the Russian Federation.

These lands include high mountains and frozen snowy plains known as tundra. The topsoil of the tundra melts in the brief northern summer, and wildflowers blossom amongst the pools of water. At midsummer the Arctic stays light for 24 hours of the day, and at midwinter the

▲ *The caribou*
This reindeer migrates across forests and tundra in vast herds. It is still hunted by the peoples of the American Arctic.

night is endless. Whales, seals, walruses and polar bears swim in the rich Arctic seas.

Many peoples have settled in the Arctic, traditionally living by hunting and fishing or by herding reindeer. Today some of them work in oil production or fish processing factories. Arctic peoples include the Aleuts of Alaska, the Inuit communities of northern Canada and Greenland (Kalaallit), the Saami of northern Scandinavia, the Evenks, Chukchi, Yukagirs, Khants, Nenets and many other groups of the Russian Federation.

▼ *Dried fish*
Fish are preserved by natural drying in many communities. Cod, Arctic char and capelin are all caught in polar waters.

Country	Area sq km	Population millions	Capital	Economy 1997
EUROPE: The Far North p.13				
Denmark	43,075	5.3	Copenhagen	bacon, butter
Finland	337,030	5.1	Helsinki	timber, paper
Iceland	103,000	0.3	Reykjavik	fish
Norway	323,895	4.4	Oslo	oil, timber, fish
Sweden	449,790	8.9	Stockholm	steel, paper
Other territories: Faeroe Islands, Jan Mayen, Svalbard				
EUROPE: Low Countries p.17				
Belgium	30,520	10.2	Brussels	steel, textiles
Luxembourg	2,585	0.4	Luxembourg	steel, banking
Netherlands	41,160	15.6	Amsterdam	dairy, bulbs
EUROPE: The British Isles p.21				
Republic of Ireland	68,895	3.6	Dublin	dairy, beer
United Kingdom of Great Britain & Northern Ireland				
England	130,360	49	London	foods, cars
Scotland	78,750	5	Edinburgh	oil, whisky
Wales	20,760	3	Cardiff	lamb, tourism
N Ireland	14,150	2	Belfast	machinery
Total	244,755	59		finance
Other territories: Isle of Man, Guernsey, Jersey				
EUROPE: France and Monaco p.25				
France	543,965	58.6	Paris	wine, fashion
Monaco	1.9	028	Monaco	chemicals
EUROPE: Germany and the Alps p.29				
Austria	83,855	8.1	Vienna	timber, tourism
Germany	356,840	82	Berlin	cars, finance
Liechtenstein	160	0.03	Vaduz	tourism
Switzerland	41,285	7.1	Bern	cheese, banking
EUROPE: The Iberian Peninsula p.33				
Andorra	465	0.06	Andorra la Viella	tourism
Portugal	91,630	9.9	Lisbon	wine, tourism
Spain	504,880	39.3	Madrid	wine, tourism
Other territories: Gibraltar				
EUROPE: Italy and its Neighbours p.37				
Italy	301,245	57.4	Rome	wine, cars
Malta	316	0.4	Valletta	dockyards

FACTS ABOUT COUNTRIES

Country	Area sq km	Population millions	Capital	Economy 1997
San Marino	61	0.02	San Marino	tourism
Vatican City	0.44	0.001	Vatican City	Catholic Church

EUROPE: Central Europe p.41

Country	Area sq km	Population millions	Capital	Economy 1997
Czech Republic	78,864	10.3	Prague	beer, glass
Estonia	45,100	1.5	Tallinn	oil, timber, pork
Hungary	93,030	10.2	Budapest	fruit, wine
Latvia	63,700	2.5	Riga	machines, dairy
Lithuania	65,200	3.7	Vilnius	machines, pork
Poland	312,685	38.6	Warsaw	coal, copper
Slovakia	49,035	5.4	Bratislava	mining, foods

EUROPE: The Balkans p.45

Country	Area sq km	Population millions	Capital	Economy 1997
Albania	28,750	3.4	Tiranë	fruit, mining
Bosnia- Herzegovina	51,130	3.6	Sarajevo	garments, chemicals
Bulgaria	110,900	8.3	Sofia	tobacco, textiles
Croatia	56,540	4.8	Zagreb	machines, chemicals
Greece	131,985	10.5	Athens	tourism, shipping
Macedonia (Former Yugoslav Republic)	25,715	2.1	Skopje	food, textiles
Romania	37,500	22.5	Bucharest	petrochemicals
Slovenia	20,250	2	Ljubljana	timber, vegetables
Yugoslavia (Serbia-Montenegro)	102,170	10.6	Belgrade	textiles, steel

EUROPE/ASIA: Russia and its Neighbours p.49

Country	Area sq km	Population millions	Capital	Economy 1997
Armenia	30,000	3.8	Yerevan	fruit, nuts, mining
Azerbaijan	87,000	7.6	Baku	oil, natural gas
Belarus	208,000	10.3	Minsk	petrochemicals
Georgia	69,700	5.4	Tbilisi	food, machines
Kazakhstan	2,717,300	16.4	Almaty	oil, wool
Kyrgyzstan	198,500	4.6	Bishkek	wool, cotton
Moldova	33,700	4.3	Chisinau	food, tobacco
Russian Federation	17,078,005	147.3	Moscow	wheat, iron ore
Tajikistan	143,100	6	Dushanbe	cotton, textiles
Turkmenistan	488,100	4.6	Askhabad	oil, cotton
Ukraine	603,700	50.7	Kiev	wheat, machines
Uzbekistan	447,400	23.7	Tashkent	cotton

NORTH AND CENTRAL AMERICA: Greenland and Canada p.53

Country	Area sq km	Population millions	Capital	Economy 1997
Canada	9,922,385	30.1	Ottawa	timber, wheat

Other territories: Greenland, St Pierre & Miquelon

Country	Area sq km	Population millions	Capital	Economy 1997
NORTH AND CENTRAL AMERICA: United States of America p.57				
USA	9,363,130	267.7	Washington DC	wheat, coal, oil

NORTH AND CENTRAL AMERICA: Mexico, Central America & Caribbean p.63

Country	Area sq km	Population millions	Capital	Economy 1997
Mexico	1,972,545	95.7	Mexico City	oil, vehicles
Central Belize	22,965	0.2	Belmopan	timber, fruit
Costa Rica	50,900	3.5	San José	coffee, bananas
El Salvador	21,395	5.9	San Salvador	coffee, maize
Guatemala	108,890	11.2	Guatemala City	coffee, bananas
Honduras	112,085	5.8	Tegucigalpa	coffee, bananas
Nicaragua	148,000	4.4	Managua	coffee, cotton
Panama	78,515	2.7	Panama City	bananas, sugar
Caribbean & North Atlantic				
Antigua & Barbuda	442	0.1	Saint John's	sugar, cotton
Bahamas	13,860	0.3	Freeport	banking, tourism
Barbados	430	0.3	Bridgetown	sugar
Cuba	114,525	11.1	Havana	sugar, coffee
Dominica	751	0.1	Roseau	bananas
Dominican Republic	48,440	8.2	Santo Domingo	sugar, coffee
Grenada	345	0.1	St George's	spices
Haiti	27,750	6.6	Port-au-Prince	sugar, coffee
Jamaica	1,425	2.6	Kingston	sugar, tourism
St Kitts-Nevis	261	0.04	Basseterre	sugar, cotton
St Lucia	616	0.1	St Lucia	tourism, bananas
St Vincent & the Grenadines	389	0.1	Kingstown	bananas, copra
Trinidad & Tobago	5,130	1.3	Port-of -Spain	petrochemicals

Other territories: Anguilla, Aruba, Bermuda, British Virgin Islands, Cayman Islands, Guadeloupe, Martinique, Montserrat, Netherlands Antilles, Puerto Rico, Turks & Caicos Islands, US Virgin Islands

SOUTH AMERICA: The Northern Andes p.67

Country	Area sq km	Population millions	Capital	Economy 1997
Bolivia	1,098,580	7.8	La Paz/Sucre	coffee, tin
Colombia	1,138,915	37.4	Bogotá	coffee, emeralds
Ecuador	461,475	12	Quito	coffee, fishmeal
Peru	1,285,215	24.4	Lima	lead, fishmeal

SOUTH AMERICA: Brazil and its Neighbours p.71

Country	Area sq km	Population millions	Capital	Economy 1997
Brazil	8,511,965	160.3	Brasília	coffee, iron ore
Guyana	214,970	0.8	Georgetown	sugar, bauxite
Surinam	163,820	0.4	Paramaribo	sugar, bauxite

Country	Area sq km	Population millions	Capital	Economy 1997
Venezuela	912,045	22.6	Caracas	oil, coffee

Other territories: French Guiana

SOUTH AMERICA: Argentina and its Neighbours p.75

Argentina	2,780,090	35.6	Buenos Aires	beef, hides
Chile	736,900	14.6	Santiago	wine, fruit
Paraguay	406,750	5.1	Asunción	beef, cotton
Uruguay	76,210	3.2	Montevideo	beef, hides

Other territories: Falkland Islands (Malvinas), South Georgia & South Sandwich Islands

ASIA: South West p.79

Bahrain	661	0.6	Manamah	oil
Cyprus	9,250	0.7	Nicosia	tourism, fruit
Iran	1,648,000	67.5	Teheran	oil, carpets
Iraq	438,445	21.2	Baghdad	oil, dates
Israel	20,770	5.8	Jerusalem	fruit, vegetables
Jordan	96,000	4.4	Amman	phosphates
Kuwait	24,280	1.8	Kuwait City	oil
Lebanon	10,400	3.9	Beirut	textiles, fruit
Oman	271,950	2.3	Muscat	oil, fishing
Qatar	11,435	0.6	Doha	oil, fertilizers
Saudi Arabia	2,400,900	19.5	Riyadh	oil, dates
Syria	185,680	15	Damascus	oil, cotton
Turkey (partly in Europe)	779,450	63.7	Ankara	tobacco, textiles
United Arab Emirates (UAE)	75,150	2.3	Abu Dhabi	oil, natural gas
Yemen	527,970	15.2	San'a	oil, fishing

ASIA: India and its Neighbours p.83

Afghanistan	652,225	22.1	Kabul	carpets, gas
Bangladesh	144,000	122.2	Dhaka	jute, tea
Bhutan	46,620	0.8	Thimphu	timber, rice
India	3,166,830	969.7	Delhi	cotton, tea
Maldives	298	0.3	Malé	fishing
Nepal	141,415	22.6	Kathmandu	tourism, timber
Pakistan	803,940	137.8	Islamabad	cotton, rice
Sri Lanka	65,610	18.7	Colombo	tea, rubber

Other territories: British Indian Ocean territory

Country	Area sq km	Population millions	Capital	Economy 1997
ASIA: China and its Neighbours p.87				
China	9,597,000	1,236.7	Beijing	rice, tea, manufacture
Korea (North)	122,310	24.3	Pyongyang	coal, textiles
Korea (South)	98,445	45.9	Seoul	vehicles, manufacture
Mongolia	565,000	2.4	Ulan Bator	wool
Taiwan	35,990	21.5	Taipei	electronics, plastics
Other territories: Macao (reverts to China 1999), Paracel Islands, Spratly Islands				
ASIA: Japan p.91				
Japan	369,700	126.1	Tokyo	cars, electronics
ASIA: South East Asia p.93				
Brunei	5,765	0.3	Bandar Seri Begawan	oil, natural gas
Cambodia	181,000	11.2	Phnom Penh	rubber, timber
Indonesia	1,919,445	204.3	Jakarta	oil, rubber
Laos	236,725	5.1	Vientiane	timber, coffee
Malaysia	332,965	21	Kuala Lumpur	timber, rubber
Myanmar (Burma)	678,030	46.8	Yangon	timber, rice, rubber
Philippines	300,000	73.4	Manila	garments, electronics
Singapore	616	3.5	Singapore City	finance, shipping
Thailand	514,000	60.1	Bangkok	tourism, rice
Vietnam	329,565	75.1	Hanoi	rice, coal
AFRICA: North and West Africa p.97				
North Africa				
Algeria	2,381,745	29.8	Algiers	oil, olives
Egypt	1,000,250	64.8	Cairo	cotton, tourism
Eritrea	91, 600	3.6	Asmara	hides, gum arabic
Libya	1,759,540	5.6	Tripoli	oil
Morocco	458,730	28.2	Rabat	phosphates, dates
Tunisia	164,150	9.3	Tunis	oil, fruits, tourism
Western Sahara	252,120	0.2	El Aaiún	phosphates
Sub-Sahara				
Burkina Faso	274,122	10.9	Ouagadougou	cotton, cattle
Chad	1,284,000	7	N'Djamena	cotton, cattle
Djibouti	23,200	0.6	Djibouti	hides, port facilities
Ethiopia	1,104,300	58.7	Addis Ababa	coffee, hides
Mali	1,240,140	9.9	Bamako	cotton, peanuts
Mauritania	1,030,700	2.4	Nouakchott	gypsum, fish
Niger	1,186,410	9.8	Niamey	cattle, vegetables
Sudan	2,505,815	27.9	Khartoum	cotton, gum arabic

Country	Area sq km	Population millions	Capital	Economy 1997
West Africa				
Benin	112,620	5.9	Porto-Novo	cotton, peanuts
Cameroon	475,500	13.9	Yaoundé	cotton, peanuts
Cape Verde Islands	4,035	0.4	Praia	fish, bananas
Côte d'Ivoire	322,465	15	Abidjan	cocoa, coffee
Equatorial Guinea	28,050	0.4	Malabo	cocoa, coffee, timber
Gambia	10,690	1.2	Banjul	fish, peanuts
Ghana	238,305	18.1	Accra	gold, cocoa
Guinea	245,855	7.5	Conakry	bauxite, coffee
Guinea-Bissau	36,125	0.1	Bissau	fish, peanuts
Liberia	111,370	2.3	Monrovia	diamonds, palm-oil
Nigeria	923,850	107.1	Abuja	oil, cotton, peanuts
Senegal	196,720	8.8	Dakar	fish, peanuts
Sierra Leone	72,325	4.4	Freetown	diamonds, cocoa
Togo	56,785	4.7	Lomé	phosphates, cotton

AFRICA: Central, Eastern and Southern Africa p.101

Country	Area sq km	Population millions	Capital	Economy 1997
Central Africa				
Burundi	27,835	6.1	Bujumbura	coffee, tea
Central African Republic	624,975	.3	Bangui	cotton, timber
Congo	342,000	2.6	Brazzaville	cocoa, timber
Congo (Democratic Republic, formerly Zaïre)	2,345,410	47.4	Kinshasa	diamonds, copper
Gabon	267,665	1.2	Libreville	oil, timber
Rwanda	26,330	7.7	Kigali	coffee, tea
São Tomé and Príncipe	964	0.1	São Tomé	cocoa, bananas
Eastern Africa				
Comoros	1,860	0.6	Moroni	copra, spices, fish
Kenya	582,645	28.8	Nairobi	tourism, coffee
Seychelles	404	0.1	Victoria	tourism, copra, fish
Somalia	637,660	10.2	Mogadishu	livestock, bananas
Tanzania	939,760	29.5	Dodoma	tourism, sisal, cloves
Uganda	236,580	20.6	Kampala	coffee, cotton
Southern Africa				
Angola	1,246,700	11.6	Luanda	coffee, diamonds
Botswana	575,000	1.5	Gaborone	cattle, hides
Lesotho	30,345	2	Maseru	wool, cattle
Madagascar	594,180	14.1	Antananarivo	coffee, spices, sugar
Malawi	94,080	9.6	Lilongwe	tobacco, cotton
Mauritius	1,865	1.1	Port Louis	sugar, tea, garments

Country	Area sq km	Population millions	Capital	Economy 1997
Mozambique	784,755	18.4	Maputo	cashew nuts, cotton
Namibia	824,295	1.7	Windhoek	uranium, diamonds
South Africa	1,220,845	42.5	Cape Town, Pretoria	gold, diamonds
Swaziland	17,365	1	Mbabane	fruit, sugar
Zambia	752,615	9.4	Lusaka	copper, lead, tobacco
Zimbabwe	390,310	11.4	Harare	tobacco, vegetables

Atlantic Ocean territories: St Helena & dependencies

Indian Ocean territories: Mayotte, Réunion

OCEANIA: Australia p.105

Australia	7,682,300	18.5	Canberra	wool, minerals, tourism

Other territories: Ashmore & Cartier Islands, Christmas Island, Cocos (Keeling) Islands, Coral sea Islands, Heard & Macdonald Islands, Norfolk Island

OCEANIA: New Zealand and the Pacific p.109

Federated States of				
Micronesia	702	0.1	Kolonia	copra, fishing
Fiji	18,330	0.8	Suva	sugar, fishing
Kiribati	684	0.025	Bairiki	copra, fishing
Marshall Islands	181	0.1	Majuro	copra, phosphates
Nauru	21	0.01	Yaren	phosphates
New Zealand	265,150	3.6	Wellington	meat, wool, fruit
Palau	490	0.02	Koror	copra, fishing
Papua New Guinea	462,840	4.4	Port Moresby	coffee, cocoa, copper
Solomon Islands	29,790	0.4	Honiara	copra, fishing
Tonga	699	0.1	Nukualofa	copra, vanilla
Tuvalu	24	0.013	Funafuti	copra, fishing
Vanuatu	14,765	0.2	Porta-Vila	copra, livestock
Western Samoa	2,840	0.2	Apia	copra, fishing

Pacific territories: American Samoa, Baker & Howard islands, Cook Islands, French Polynesia, Guam, Jarvis Island, Johnston Atoll, Kingman Reef, Midway Islands, New Caledonia, Niue, Northern Marianas, Pitcairn, Tokelau, Wake Island, Wallis & Futuna

Southern ocean territories: Bouvet Island, French Southern & Antarctic Territories

INDEX

Acknowledgements

The publishers would like to thank the following artists who contributed to this book:

Julie Banyard, Janos Marffy, Josephine Martin, Terry Riley, Guy Smith and Michael White.

Our thanks to Keith Lye for the use of his photographs on pages 68 (B/L); 79 (B/L); 80 (C); 81 (B); 84 (T/R); 88 (T/L); 97 (T/L); 98 (T/L)

Other photographs are from MKP Archives.